GERMAN AUTUMN

GERMAN AUTUMN

STIG DAGERMAN

Foreword by Mark Kurlansky
Translated by Robin Fulton Macpherson

University of Minnesota Press
Minneapolis

First published as *Tysk Höst* by Norstedts, Sweden, in 1947; copyright 1947 Stig Dagerman.

First published in English in Great Britain by Quartet Books Limited, 1988

First U.S. edition published by the University of Minnesota Press, 2011, by agreement with Norstedts Agency.

English translation and Introduction copyright 1988 by Robin Fulton Macpherson

Foreword copyright 2011 by the Regents of the University of Minnesota

Published by the University of Minnesota Press
111 Third Avenue South, Suite 290
Minneapolis, MN 55401-2520
http://www.upress.umn.edu

Library of Congress Cataloging-in-Publication Data

Dagerman, Stig, 1923–1954.
[Tysk höst. English]
 German autumn / Stig Dagerman, foreword by Mark Kurlansky, translated by Robin Fulton Macpherson. — 1st U.S. ed. p. cm.
 ISBN 978-0-8166-7752-8 (pb : alk. paper)
 1. Germany—History—1945–1955. 2. Germany—Social life and customs—20th century. 3. Germany—Intellectual life—20th century. I. Macpherson, Robin Fulton. II. Title.
 PT9875.D1213 2011
 839.78'7403—dc23

2011030476

CONTENTS

FOREWORD

Pitiless Fall

MARK KURLANSKY

Doomed be the fatherland, false name,
Where nothing thrives but disgrace and shame
—Heinrich Heine, *Germany: A Winter's Tale* (1844)

There is a place I like to go on the Upper East Side of Manhattan. It is the Neue Galerie, a museum specializing in the art of Germany and Austria, much of it from what was a kind of golden age during the first part of the twentieth century. A gift shop features Austro-German design from the early twentieth century, and the bookstore sells German literature in German and translated into English (Goethe, Heine, Mann, and the great thinkers—Freud, Hegel, Spengler, Kant, Nietzsche, Marx, Jaspers), as well as books about the artists and the great expressionist filmmakers who influenced directors such as Alfred Hitchcock. Then I sit in the café, where they serve Riesling wine in little carafes (fruity but not the cheap postwar sugared variety) and spätzle and sausage and light crispy apfelstrudel with an imposing cloud of whipped cream, all consumed while listening to Mozart with some well-dressed older people at other tables whispering in the wonderfully expressive

vii

German language—a language that seems designed for expanding ideas. I sit there and think, this is what it would be like, this is how we would think of Germany, if Adolf Hitler had not come to power.

American schoolchildren used to study German. It was the leading second language before Hitler came to power. Even after World War I, my parents, Jewish kids, studied German in school. Germany was one of the great centers of European culture. But Hitler did come to power, and we have never thought of Germany the same way since.

A number of notable German intellectuals predicted that out of the richness of German thought would come an arrogance that would destroy Germany. In 1834 the poet Heinrich Heine wrote, "German thunder is of true Germanic character; it is not very nimble, but rumbles along ponderously. Yet, it will come and when you hear a crashing such as never before has been heard in the world's history, then you know that the German thunderbolt has fallen at last. At that uproar the eagles of the air will drop dead, and lions in the remotest deserts of Africa will hide in their royal dens. A play will be performed in Germany that will make the French Revolution look like an innocent idyll."

In 1889, Nietzsche wrote, "I know my fate. One day there will be associated with my name the recollection of something frightful—of a crisis like no other before on earth." The crisis came and was associated with his name though most historians believe that Hitler's claim even to have read Nietzsche was a lie.

In his novel *The Magic Mountain* (1924), Thomas Mann wrote, "Passion means to live life for life's sake. But I am well aware you Germans live it for the sake of experience. Passion means to forget oneself. But you do things in order to enrich yourselves. *C'est ça.* You haven't the least notion how repulsively egoistic that is of you and that someday it may well make you the enemy of humankind."

By 1945 Hitler was dead and Germany was physically, morally, psychologically, and spiritually in ruins. Not only was the German claim to civilization gone, but most of the world did regard Germans as "the enemy of humankind" and unworthy of even basic human compassion.

In 1946 Thomas Mann, then considered Germany's greatest modern writer and an opponent of the regime, stated that even the German language had lost credibility: "To be a German author— what will that be? Back of every sentence that we construct in our language stands a broken, a spiritually burnt-out people, bewildered about itself and its history, a people that, according to reports, despairs of ever governing itself." Mann called Germans "a people that can never show its face again."

That same year, in the autumn of 1946, Stig Dagerman, wunderkind of Swedish letters at the age of twenty-three, was sent to Germany by the Swedish newspaper *Expressen*. Dagerman was a too-bright filament that burned out quickly. He had already written two novels and been proclaimed in Sweden as the premier genius of a new generation. The year after he wrote *German Autumn* he would publish a collection of short stories and his first play was produced in Stockholm to dazzling success. The next year he wrote two more plays and a third novel. The next year he came out with a fourth novel and wrote a fourth play. Except for this last play, which the author himself disliked, all of these works, including *German Autumn*, were widely regarded as brilliant.

But then he couldn't write anymore.

Dagerman was twenty-six and used up. He undertook projects, he kept trying, but he could not write. In 1954, age thirty-one, he gassed himself to death in his car parked in his garage. Recent research suggests he may have been suffering from clinical depression or bipolar disorder with possible manic episodes.

Dagerman's extraordinary gift was his ability to empathize. He came from a poor rural background; his grandparents raise him because he was abandoned by his parents. A deranged man stabbed his grandfather to death, and his grandmother died soon after from the shock. When Dagerman heard of the murder he tried to write a poem about his feelings. He couldn't do it, but he regarded that experience as his beginning as a writer. "Something was born," he wrote. "Something that I believe was the desire to be a writer; that is to say, to be able to tell of what it is to mourn, to have been loved, to be left lonely . . . " He said his grandmother had "the courage to show love." Stig Dagerman had the courage to show compassion, and in Germany in 1946 that required a considerable amount of courage.

The Allied bombing of Germany and Japan during World War II demonstrated the classic example of the old argument of war resisters that if you go to war you start to resemble your enemy.

Until the beginning of the Allied campaigns the overwhelming opinion in the nations that were carrying out this bombing (principally Britain and the United States, but also world opinion in general) was that dropping explosives on a civilian population from airplanes was a heinous crime. On April 26, 1937, German and Italian planes firebombed Guernica, the historic capital of Basque country in northern Spain. The world was outraged by this new form of warfare, random attacks on civilian populations from the air. The raid was seen as proof of the brutality of fascism.

Then, with little protest, these same outraged nations conducted a bombing campaign that killed an estimated 300,000 German civilians and wounded more than 800,000 Germans. This is a modest estimate; in Europe and Asia combined, Allied bombing is thought to have killed at least 800,000 people. The question is whether it is morally relevant to point out that although German bombing killed only a fraction of this total, the Germans did kill millions of civilians, including the six million systematically exterminated in specifically designed death camps. So how can we feel sorry for them?

But what had happened to the values of the people who had been outraged about Guernica? The problem was once explained by President Dwight D. Eisenhower, the former Allied commander who declared in a press conference in 1955 that once you get into a war you get "deeper and deeper" until the only obstacles are the limitations of "force itself."

As is pointed out in an almost childlike way, the Germans started it. They started it not only in Durango and Guernica during the Spanish Civil War but with their nearly twelve-hour bombing on November 15, 1940, of the historic English city of Coventry, in which six hundred civilians, the center of the city, and a famous fourteenth-century cathedral were destroyed. The Germans issued a statement that this occurred in reprisal for British RAF raids on German cities, which had been ongoing since May.

The British raids had been primarily military targets, but after Coventry that changed. They began targeting the center of cities regardless of their military importance. Working-class neighborhoods were particularly sought for destruction. The strategy was to destroy German morale, an odd decision considering that the German attacks on Coventry and London were stiffening the resolve of the British. And though Winston Churchill presented the bombing campaign as well-deserved revenge, polls showed that the British people had reservations, especially in places that had been attacked, such as London. These reservations existed despite the fact that most British people did not know the extent to which German civilians were being targeted.

These were raids of unprecedented brutality. According to the highest, and probably most accurate, estimate (that of the Basque government), 1,645 Basque civilians were killed in the attack on Guernica that stunned the world. But there was no outcry after the bombing of Cologne on June 28–29, 1943, in which 4,377 German civilians were killed, or the July 27–28 raid on Hamburg in which 35,000 German civilians were killed and 800,000 homes destroyed. It was constant: by 1944 a city was bombed in Germany almost every day. An estimated 10,550 civilians died on the raid on Darmstadt on September 11–12, 1944. On January 16–17, 1945, 16,000 civilians died in a raid on Magdeburg; on February 3, 2,541 Germans were killed in Berlin and nearly 120,000 homes destroyed. Most famously, on February 13–14, it is estimated that more than 30,000 civilians were killed (other estimates go as high as 100,000 or more) in a raid on Dresden that included a bombing technique that caused a wall of fire to rush through the streets and burn—even melt—the entire inner city. The Allies became increasingly efficient at this kind of destruction. Dresden was a joint British–American operation. Once the United States joined the war in 1942, it joined the bombing campaign.

Some military officers questioned the strategy and feared that by targeting civilians rather than shipyards, factories, and other military targets, they were actually lengthening the war. Rear Admiral L. H. K. Hamilton expressed it in practical terms: "We are a hopelessly unmilitary nation to imagine that we win the war by bombing German women and children instead of defeating their army and navy." But others, such as Sir Arthur Harris, the chief of British Bomber Command, were certain they would destroy Germany's spirit, all evidence to the contrary. Harris even objected to diverting his bombers from civilian targets in the heartland to support the Normandy invasion.

When Heinrich Heine returned from exile in France in 1843 he found Hamburg shattered from war damage and described it as "a poodle halfway shorn." When Dagerman arrived in 1946 such flippancy would have been unimaginable because in the intervening hundred years the human capacity for destruction had greatly advanced. Dagerman described Hamburg as "a landscape of ruins drearier than the desert, wilder than a mountain-top, and as far-fetched as a nightmare." That same year Mann had warned, "It is impossible to demand of the abused nations of Europe, of the world, that they shall draw a neat dividing line between 'Nazism' and the German people."

Dagerman didn't try. He was not neutral: he had a history of active antifascism from his teenage years, when most of the world was not speaking out against the new German regime. But he did not consider passing judgment on these people part of his role. He was a young man who understood deprivation, hunger, and loss. These were human beings who had lost everything, who were living in the flooded, chilly basements of bombed-out buildings, looking for scraps of food. Journalists working in Germany found a strong vein of Nazi sentiment, and Dagerman found such people as well, but he criticized journalists for regarding "the Germans as one solid block, irradiating Nazi chill, and not as a multitude of starving and freezing individuals." Dagerman found, in the words of Holocaust historian Raul Hilberg, perpetrators, victims, and by-standers—concentration camp survivors and SS members all crawling through the same rubble, all people in deplorable conditions.

Dagerman's compassion was no small accomplishment. On my many trips to Germany I have always sought out the victims, discovered a few perpetrators, and been deeply disturbed by the knowledge that most of the people I saw were bystanders. I felt as Mann wrote that "the lack of a sense of the evil of the obviously and unequivocally wicked will always be a crime"—an unforgiveable one. Twenty-five years after Dagerman's German autumn I was on a transatlantic ship (they were still transportation then), and a suave, silver-haired man from Munich standing at a bar said to me that "the fire bombing of Dresden was the greatest atrocity of World War II." I did not want to speak to this man again. He had actually lived through the Nazi years in Germany and thought the Allied bombing, horrendous as it was, was the greatest atrocity.

Twenty years later I was in Dresden, the center still in ruins, reporting on the efforts of the newly unified Germany to at last rebuild that historic baroque city. Dresdeners tried to evoke my sympathy, but they kept leading me to archives that showed the destruction and what it was like before. *Before* was the problem—all those photographs of plump and happy Germans cheering swastikaed mass murderers. This is not easily overlooked and I'm not sure it should be overlooked. But Dagerman understood what was at stake. He quoted Victor Gollancz, a Jewish publisher in London who had only recently made his own visit to Germany that autumn and warned that "the values of the West are in danger." Gollancz, a far more active antifascist than Dagerman and one of the few to speak loudly of the Holocaust during the war, was so disturbed by the conditions he found in Germany that he published that year a book about it, *Our Threatened Values.* Like Gollancz, Dagerman believed that compassion had to be preserved, that it was vital to maintain "the capacity to react in the face of suffering whether that suffering may be deserved or undeserved."

Had we listened, had we felt more compassion, had we felt more troubled by the human suffering that was caused by our bombs, perhaps we would have spoken out louder and not ourselves been bystanders to the bombing of Hanoi and of Baghdad. World War II had been more brutal to civilians than warfare had ever been before. In the wars since then, the percentage of civilians on the conflict's casualty list has been steadily rising.

German Autumn is a very important book and it is crucial that an English language version is now available for Americans. We need this book. Karl Jaspers, the German psychiatrist turned philosopher, wrote, "We wish to understand history as a whole, in order to understand ourselves."

New York City
June 2011

INTRODUCTION

In his study of Stig Dagerman (1958) Olof Lagercrantz quotes from
a letter Dagerman wrote from Munich to his friend and colleague
Werner Aspenström:

> A journalist I have not yet become, and it doesn't look as if I'll
> ever be one. I have no wish to acquire all the deplorable
> attributes that go to make up a perfect journalist. I find it hard to
> understand the people I meet at the Allied Press hotel – they
> think that a small hunger-strike is more interesting than the
> hunger of multitudes. While hunger-riots are sensational, hunger
> itself is not sensational, and what poverty-stricken and bitter
> people here think becomes interesting only when poverty and
> bitterness break out in a catastrophe. Journalism is the art of
> coming too late as early as possible. I'll never master that.

In fact Dagerman was a very effective journalist of the kind he
wanted to be. When the Swedish newspaper *Expressen* asked him
to go to Germany in the autumn of 1946 and write articles about
what he saw there, he was by no means unqualified for the task: he
knew the language (his first wife was German) and he had already
had some journalistic and editorial experience on various papers
and journals of the time (notably the Syndicalist *Arbetaren*). He
may well have had deeper motives for seeking out people in
extreme situations. We cannot tell how explicit these may have
been, but I think it is mistaken to see *German Autumn* as marginal
to his more 'literary' productions: the book touches on some of his
basic concerns, and the process of writing it could well have proved
a useful exercise in observation and realistic description.

1

The articles were duly written and published, and were made into a book the following year. Undoubtedly this helped to further Dagerman's already growing reputation. It attracted, and still deserves, attention partly because he had a sharp eye for concrete details, partly because he could argue pungently, but mainly because he dared to see German individuals as suffering human beings rather than simply as tokens of national disgrace or guilt.

And it was this that brought him into conflict with the kind of journalism he often found practised by so many Allied reporters and other foreign investigators. They may have called themselves 'observers' but to Dagerman they refused to use their eyes. 'A French journalist of high repute begged me with the best of intentions and for the sake of objectivity to read German newspapers instead of looking at German dwellings or sniffing in German cooking-pots.'

At one level some of their responses simply irritated him. So many times it was said or written that the conditions in which countless Germans had to live were 'indescribable'. That is nonsense, said Dagerman: 'If one wants to describe them, they can be described quite perfectly.' And he went on to describe them. On the political level he was sceptical of the Allies' ability or will to help the Germans eradicate Nazism: he felt that Allied tactics 'helped to make the soil for democracy more sterile rather than more favourable'. 'Denazification' he saw as a cynical farce which by and large eased the transition into civilian life for ex-Nazis, often at the expense of those they had previously oppressed. He derided those journalists who asked people who lived in waterlogged cellars if life had been better under Hitler and then affected horror when the answer was 'Yes'. 'If you ask someone starving on two slices of bread per day if he was better off when he was starving on five you will doubtless get the same answer.'

At a deeper level questions of guilt and suffering gnaw at Dagerman throughout the journey. His greatest contempt is for the naïve and cruel notion that the German people as a whole 'deserve' their suffering. He responds not with abstract arguments but by looking at the lives of the people he meets. Does deserved suffering feel any different from undeserved suffering? What happens to people who are permanently hungry? 'For hunger is a form of unaccountability, not just a physical but also a mental state that leaves minimum space for the leisure of thought. This meant that one naturally heard things which sounded most unattractive but

2

which, nevertheless, in the given situation, gave one no right to make cocksure prognoses.'

From the ex-Nazi prosecutor who survives Year Zero with plenty of firewood and whose children eat real butter, and the writer-aesthete who withdraws into history, there is an extraordinary range of individual fates. To those who were suffering Dagerman allows a degree of respect, a kind of prerogative, that qualifies whatever judgements he may be inclined to make. He never forgets that the comparative luxury of the Press hotel ('No German Civilians') is waiting for him. And when he leaves, he is well aware of the privileged nature of his voluntary expedition into the landscapes of ruin and want. One question, he tells us, weighed on him more than any other: 'What would it be like to have to stay behind, to have to be hungry every day, to have to sleep in a cellar, to fight at every moment against the temptation to steal, to have to tremble with cold every minute, to have to survive, constantly, the most intractable conditions? I remember people I met who had to tolerate almost all of that.'

But the book does not end with such a neat gesture. Dagerman leaves us in his last chapter with a gallery of individual experiences, true stories of how people he met responded to the process of survival and recovery – a gallery of enigmas, we could say, as if Dagerman were defying us to think of easy conclusions about whether this or that person was simply right or simply wrong. It is not by accident that the last person mentioned is a camp-survivor who sees no point in trying to tell his story.

German Autumn

In the autumn of 1946 the leaves were falling in Germany for the third time since Churchill's famous speech about the falling of leaves. It was a gloomy season with rain, cold – and hunger, especially in the Ruhr and generally throughout the rest of the old Third Reich. All autumn, trains arrived in the Western Zones with refugees from the Eastern Zone. Ragged, starving and unwelcome, they crowded in dark, stinking station-bunkers or in the giant windowless bunkers that look like rectangular gasometers, looming like huge monuments to defeat in Germany's collapsed cities. The silence and passive submission of these apparently insignificant people gave a sense of dark bitterness to that German autumn. They became significant just because they came and never stopped coming and because they came in such numbers. They became significant perhaps not in spite of their silence but because of it, for nothing can be expressed with such a charge of menace as that which is not expressed. Their presence was both hateful and welcome – hateful because they arrived bringing with them nothing but their hunger and their thirst, welcome because it fed suspicions which one would willingly entertain, distrust which one would willingly cultivate, and despair by which one would willingly be possessed.

And can anyone who actually experienced that German autumn say that this distrust was not justified or that this despair was unmotivàted? It can well be said that these never-thinning streams of refugees that flowed across the German lowlands from the lower Rhine and the lower Elbe as far as the windy highlands around Munich were one of the most important factors in the internal affairs of this country without internal affairs. Another factor of domestic policy, and of about the same significance, was the rain that lay two feet deep in the populated cellars of the Ruhr district.

Someone wakens, if she has slept at all, freezing in a bed without blankets, and wades over the ankles in cold water to the stove and tries to coax some fire out of some sour branches from a bombed tree. Somewhere in the water behind, tuberculous children are hoarsely coughing. If she does succeed in getting a few flames going in the stove – a stove which at the risk of her life she has heaved out of a crumbling ruin which its owner has lain buried several yards beneath for the past two years – the smoke billows into the cellar and those who are already coughing cough even more. On the stove there is a pan of water (there is no lack of water) and she stoops and gropes in the water on the floor and plucks up some potatoes that have been lying invisible beneath the surface. The woman standing ankle-deep in cold water puts these potatoes in the pan and waits for them until, in due course, they are edible, although they were already frozen when she managed to get hold of them.

Doctors who talk to foreign interviewers about the eating habits of these families say that what they boil up in their pans is indescribable. It is not indescribable at all, any more than their whole manner of existing is indescribable. The anonymous meat which in one way or another they come across, or the dirty vegetables which they find God knows where, are profoundly unsavoury, but the unsavoury is not indescribable – only unsavoury. We can in the same way meet the objection that the sufferings which the children in these cellar-pools must undergo are indescribable. If one wants to describe them, they can be described quite perfectly – in the following way, for instance: the woman standing in the water by the stove leaves the cooking to its fate, crosses to the bed where the three coughing children lie and orders them to get off to school at once. Smoke, cold and hunger fill the cellar, and the children, who have slept fully clothed, step into the water, which laps almost over the tops of their tattered shoes, and make their way through the dark passage-way where people are sleeping, up the dark stairs where people are sleeping, and out into the chilly, wet German autumn. School does not begin for two hours yet, and the teachers tell foreign visitors about the cruelty of the parents who drive their children out on to the street. But one could argue with those teachers on the question of what kindness in this case would consist of. The Nazi aphorist wrote about the kindness of the executioner as seen in his quick, or perhaps in his well-aimed, stroke. The kindness of these parents is to be seen in the fact that they drive their children out from the water indoors to the rain out of doors, from the raw damp of the cellar to the greyness of the street.

7

Of course they do not go to school, partly because the school is not open, partly because 'going to school' is just one of those euphemisms created by necessity for those in need. They go out to steal, or to try to come across something edible by means innocent or otherwise. One could describe the 'indescribable' wanderings of these three children in the morning hours before school properly begins and then give a series of 'indescribable' pictures of their classroom activities: how slates are nailed over the windows to keep out the cold, but how these also keep out the light so a lamp has to be kept on all day but with such a dull effect that it is only with the greatest difficulty that the pupils can read whatever they are supposed to copy; how the view from the playground is surrounded on three sides by high piles of rubble (standard international variety) and how these piles of rubble also serve as school lavatories.

At the same time it would be proper to describe the 'indescribable' activities with which those who stay at home in their water fill their day; or the 'indescribable' feelings of the mother of the three hungry children when they ask her why she does not paint herself like Auntie Schulze and then get chocolate and cigarettes and tins of food from an Allied soldier. And the honesty and the moral degradation in that waterlogged cellar are both so 'indescribable' that this mother replies that not even the soldiers of a liberating army are so full of charity that they would put up with a dirty, worn-out and soon ageing body when the city is full of younger, stronger and cleaner bodies.

There is no doubt then that this autumn cellar was an element of the greatest consequence in the domestic politics of the time. So were the grass, the bushes and the mosses which gave a green shading to the piles of ruins in places like Düsseldorf and Hamburg. (For the third year in succession Herr Schumann walks past the ruins of the neighbouring block on his way to his work at the bank and every day he argues with his wife and his colleagues whether this greenery is to be considered as progress or decline.) The white faces of people now in their fourth year of bunker-life and so strikingly reminiscent of fish when they come up for a snatch of air, and the startlingly red faces of certain girls who several times a month are favoured with bars of chocolate, a carton of Chesterfields, fountain-pens or cakes of soap – these were readily observed facts which set their mark (although to a decreasing extent as the situation caused by the steady arrival of refugees worsened) on the previous German winter, spring and summer.

Drawing up an account is naturally rather a sad business, especially if it is sad things that must be counted, but in certain cases it has to be done. If any commentary is to be risked on the mood of bitterness towards the Allies, mixed with self-contempt, with apathy, with comparisons to the disadvantage of the present – all of which were certain to strike the visitor that gloomy autumn – it is necessary to keep in mind a whole series of particular occurrences and physical conditions. It is important to remember that statements implying dissatisfaction with or even distrust of the goodwill of the victorious democracies were made not in an airless room or on a theatrical stage echoing with ideological repartee but in all too palpable cellars in Essen, Hamburg or Frankfurt-am-Main. Our autumn picture of the family in the waterlogged cellar also contains a journalist who, carefully balancing on planks set across the water, interviews the family on their views of the newly reconstituted democracy in their country, asks about their hopes and illusions, and, above all, asks if the family was better off under Hitler. The answer that the visitor then receives has this result: stooping with rage, nausea and contempt, the journalist scrambles hastily backwards out of the stinking room, jumps into his hired English car or American jeep, and half an hour later over a drink or a good glass of real German beer in the bar of the Press hotel composes a report on the subject 'Nazism is alive in Germany'.

The picture of the German state of mind in this third autumn which was conveyed to the outside world by this and many other journalists and foreign visitors and which thus became the general property of that outside world was of course in its way correct. They asked cellar-Germans if they had been better off under Hitler and these Germans replied: 'Yes'. If you ask a drowning man if he was better off when he was standing up on the quay the drowning man will reply: 'Yes'. If you ask someone starving on two slices of bread per day if he was better off when he was starving on five you will doubtless get the same answer. Each analysis of the ideological position of the German people during this difficult autumn will be deeply misleading if it does not at the same time convey a sufficiently indelible picture of the milieu, of the way of life to which these human beings under analysis were condemned. A French journalist of high repute begged me with the best of intentions and for the sake of objectivity to read German newspapers instead of looking at German dwellings or sniffing in German cooking-pots. Is it not something of this attitude which colours a large part of world opinion and which made Victor Gollancz, the Jewish publisher from London, feel, after his journey to Germany in this same autumn, that 'the values of the West are in danger' – values consisting of respect for the individual even when the individual has forfeited our sympathy and compassion, that is, the capacity to react in the face of suffering whether that suffering may be deserved or undeserved.

People hear voices saying that things were better before, but they isolate these voices from the circumstances in which their owners find themselves and they listen to them in the same way as we listen to voices on the radio. They call this objectivity because they lack the imagination to visualize these circumstances and indeed, on the grounds of moral decency, they would reject such an imagination because it would appeal to an unreasonable degree of sympathy. People analyse; in fact it is a kind of blackmail to analyse the political leanings of the hungry without at the same time analysing hunger.

Of the cruelties of the past practised by Germans in and out of Germany, there can be only one opinion, since of cruelty in general, of whatever kind and whoever practises it, there can be only one opinion. But it is another matter to ask if it is now right, if it is not indeed a cruelty, to regard the sufferings of the Germans as justified on the ground that they are the undoubted results of a German war of aggression that failed. Even from a judicial point of view such an argument is quite untenable because the German distress is collective whereas the German

11

cruelties were, despite everything, not so. Further, hunger and cold are not included among the indictable offences of legal justice, for the same reason that torture and abuse are not, and a moral judgement that condemns the accused to an inhuman existence – that is to an existence which lowers rather than raises the human worth of those who are judged – denies what ought to be the unspoken object of earthly justice and has itself removed the basis for its right to exist.

The principle of guilt and retribution could acquire at least an appearance of justification if those in judgement were themselves to adhere to a principle directly contrary to that which has resulted in this autumn's being for most Germans a cold, rainy and ruinous hell. That is not the case: the collective accusation directed at the German people involves obedience *in absurdum*, obedience even in cases where disobedience would have been the only humanly justified response. But isn't obedience itself ultimately what designates the individual's relation to authority in every state in the world? Not even in the mildest of authoritarian states can it be avoided that the citizen's duty of obedience to the state may collide with his duty of love or respect for those closest to him (the bailiff who throws a family's furniture on the street, the officer who lets a subordinate die in a battle that does not concern him). What is, in the last resort, essential is the recognition in principle of the enforcement of obedience. Once this is admitted then it is soon clear that the state which demands obedience has at its disposal the means of compelling obedience even in the refractory. Obedience to the state is indivisible.

The journalist who backed out of the waterlogged

cellar in the Ruhr is therefore, to the extent that his reaction is conditioned by conscious moral principle, an immoral person, a hypocrite. He considers himself a realist, but no one is less of a realist than he is. With his own ears he has heard the hungry family say that they were better off under Hitler. When he has heard many other families in many other and perhaps somewhat more habitable cellars and rooms make the same admission he draws the conclusion that the German people are still infected by Nazism. His lack of realism here consists in the fact that he regards the Germans as one solid block, irradiating Nazi chill, and not as a multitude of starving and freezing individuals. He is particularly offended by the answer to his elaborate question because he considers it the duty of the German cellar-people to extract political lessons from the damp of their cellars, from TB, from the lack of food, clothes and warmth: the lesson that Hitler's politics and their own participation in the way they were carried out caused their ruin, and brought them down to this waterlogged cellar. Whatever the truth of this, the mere presentation of the matter in such terms indicates an absence of both realism and psychological insight.

People demanded of those who were suffering their way through this German autumn that they should learn from their misfortune. No one thought that hunger is a very bad teacher. Anyone who is properly hungry, and helplessly so, does not upbraid himself for his own hunger: instead, he upbraids those from whom he thinks he could have expected help. Nor does hunger encourage investigation into the web of causes: anyone who is permanently hungry does not have the strength to find connections beyond the most immediate, which means in this case that he upbraids those who brought down the regime which previously met his needs and who are now meeting those needs less adequately than he was accustomed to.

This is of course not a particularly 'moral' line of thought, but hunger has nothing to do with morality. *'Erst kommt das Fressen, dann die Moral ...'* The *Threepenny Opera* was staged in various places in Germany during this autumn and was met with enthusiasm, but with a different kind of enthusiasm from before: what had been seething social criticism, a pungent open letter calling for social responsibility, was transformed into a celebration of social irresponsibility.

War is an equally inept teacher. When one tried to quizz the cellar-German on what the war had taught him, the answer was not – alas – that it had taught him to hate and despise the regime that had brought it about, for the simple fact is that perpetual fear of death has only two things to teach: to be afraid and to die.

The situation in which the visitor in the autumn of 1946 found the German people was such that it was a moral impossibility to extract any conclusions at all about its ideological attitude. For hunger is a form of unaccountability, not just a physical but also a mental state that leaves minimum space for the leisure of thought. This meant that one naturally heard things which sounded most unattractive but which neverthe-less gave one no right to make cocksure prognoses. In my own case I heard nothing more repellent than the declaration of a Hamburg bank director who believed that the Norwegians should in spite of everything be grateful for the German occupation because it had given them a whole series of mountain-roads ...

Apathy and cynicism ('... *dann kommt die Moral*') were two conditions which marked the reaction to the two most important political events – the executions in Nuremberg and the first free elections. The people of Hamburg stood in grey crowds before the placards announcing that the death sentences had been carried out. No one said a word. People read, and passed on. People did not even look serious, just indifferent. True enough, in a girls' high school in Wuppertal the pupils wore mourning on 15 October; in Hamburg during the night someone had painted '*Shame Nürnberg*' in huge letters; and in an underground station in front of a poster showing a bombing raid a man grasped my arm and hissed: 'Those who did that won't be condemned.' But the exceptions only stressed the general indifference. In a deathly silent Berlin, 20 October, the first day of the free elections, looked like all the other dead Sundays. There was not the slightest trace of enthusiasm or joy in the crowds of deathly silent voters.

Throughout that autumn there were elections in various places in Germany. Participation was perhaps surprisingly active but political activity limited itself to voting. And the situation was such that conclusions based on the outcome had to be drawn with the greatest care. A Social Democratic victory and a Communist defeat – two clear facts but far from being as clear as they would be in a normal society. The Social Democratic election propaganda engaged itself strongly with foreign affairs, meaning the Soviet Union, while the Communist variety was busy with domestic problems, meaning bread. Given the

15

conditions in the cellars, it is wrong to suppose that the results indicated a democratic instinct in the German people but right to suppose that fear was patently stronger than hunger.

Just as it is wrong to draw general conclusions about the hold of Nazism on Germans on the basis of bitter sneers thrown from German cellars, so must it be equally wrong to mention the word 'democracy' in connection with the voting figures of this German autumn. If you are living at the edge of starvation then your first interest is in fighting not for democracy but to distance yourself as far as possible from that edge. The question really is whether the free elections did not come much too soon. As a training exercise in democracy they were quite meaningless because they were offset by so many significant and negative factors on the level of foreign affairs: the limited area of manoeuvre available to the politicians meant that the elections came to be regarded by the sceptics with distrust, as a tactical dodge on the part of the Allies to divert criticism of the supply situation from the Allied to the German authorities. A lightning-conductor and nothing else. The conditions for democracy consisted not in free elections but in an improved supply of provisions, an existence with hope in it. All that made this existence more hopeless – reduced rations and the contrast with the well-being of the Allied soldiers, the clumsy dismantling operations where the confiscated material was left to lie rusting in the autumn rains, the practice of making five German families homeless to make space for one Allied family, and above all the attempt to eradicate militarism by means of a military regime, to try to foster contempt for German uniforms in a country swamped by Allied uniforms – all that helped to make the soil for democracy more sterile rather than more favourable, when the latter ought to have been the obvious preference.

Briefly, the journalist who backed out of the autumn cellar should have been humbler, humble in the face of suffering, however deserved it may have been, for deserved suffering is just as heavy to bear as undeserved suffering; it is felt just as much in the stomach, in the chest, in the feet, and these three very concrete pains should not be forgotten in the raw draught of bitterness blowing from a rainy German post-war autumn.

Ruins

When every available consolation has been exhausted a new one must be invented even if it should turn out to be absurd. In German cities it often happens that people ask the stranger to confirm that their city is the most burnt, devastated and crumbled in the whole of Germany. It is not a matter of finding consolation in the midst of distress – distress itself has become a consolation. The same people become down-hearted if you tell them that you have seen worse things in other places. It may be that we have no right to say so for each German city is 'the worst' for those who have to live in it.

Berlin has its amputated spires and its endless rows of shattered government palaces, whose fallen Prussian colonnades rest their Greek profiles on the pavements. In Hannover King Ernst August sits before the station on the only fat horse in Germany and is practically the only object to have emerged unscathed in a city which once had dwellings for 450,000 people. Essen is a terrible dream-landscape of denuded, freezing iron-constructions and ravaged factory walls.

Cologne's three bridges have spent the last two years submerged in the Rhine, and the cathedral looms melancholy, sooty and alone in a pile of rubble with a fresh red wound along one side which seems to bleed at twilight. The small, black, threatening medieval towers have fallen into Nuremberg's moats, and in the small towns of the Rhineland ribs stick out of bombed timber-houses. Yet there is still a city that charges admission to a ruin: Heidelberg, which was spared the onslaught and whose beautiful old castle ruin looks like a demonic parody in an age of ruins.

Perhaps on the whole it is 'worst' everywhere. But if you have a liking for superlatives, if you want to be an expert in ruins, if you would like to have a pattern-card showing everything a wiped-out city can offer by way of crumbling walls, if you would like to see not a city of ruins but a landscape of ruins drearier than the desert, wilder than a mountain-top and as far-fetched as a nightmare, there is still only one German city that will do, and that is Hamburg.

There is an area in Hamburg that once had straight wide streets, squares with flower-beds, five-storey houses with lawns, garages, pubs, churches and all kinds of public amenities. It begins near one station on a suburban line and continues to the next station and a little beyond.

Travelling on this line you can sit for a quarter of an hour with an unbroken view of something resembling a vast dumping-ground for shattered gables, free-standing house-walls whose empty window-holes are like wide-open eyes staring down on the train, unidentifiable fragments of houses with broad black smoke-scars, tall and boldly sculptured as

20

victory monuments or small as modest gravestones.

Rusty girders poke out of the gravel-heaps like the stems of long-since foundered boats. Slender pillars which an artistic fate carved out of collapsed tenements rise from white piles of crushed bath-tubs or from grey piles of stone, powdered brick and melted radiators. Carefully manipulated façades, with nothing to be façades for, stand there like scenery for a play that was never performed.

All the figures of geometry are on display in this three-year-old variation of Guernica and Coventry: regular rectangles of school walls, small or large triangles, rhombi and ovals of the outer walls of the huge tenements that as recently as the spring of 1943 loomed between the stations of Hasselbrook and Landwehr.

Through this gigantic wasteland the train proceeds at a normal pace for about a quarter of an hour and during that time neither my silent guide nor I catch sight of a single human being in an area which was once one of Hamburg's most densely populated. The train, like all German trains, is packed full, but apart from the two of us no one looks out of the window to catch a glimpse of what is perhaps Europe's most dreadful collection of ruins. When I look round at the other passengers I meet glances that say: 'Someone who doesn't belong here.'

The stranger betrays himself immediately through his interest in ruins. Becoming immune takes time, but it does happen. My guide became immune ages ago, but she has a purely personal interest in the moonscape between Hasselbrook and Landwehr. She lived there for six years but has not seen it again since an April night in 1943 when the bombs rained over Hamburg.

We get off the train at Landwehr. I assume we must be the only people to leave the train there but we are not. There are others than tourists who have cause to come this way – there are people who live here, though this could hardly be suspected from the train window. And it is hard to realize even from the street. We walk for a while on what had been the pavements of what had been the streets and look for what had been a house but never find it. We have to circumnavigate contorted remains which on closer examination turn out to be burnt cars lying on their backs in the rubble. We look in through the gaping holes in torn houses where the girders twist like snakes down from floor to floor. We stumble over coiling water-pipes. We pause before houses where the outer wall has been ripped away, reminding us of those popular plays in which the audience can watch life being lived on several different levels simultaneously.

But here any attempt to spy out even the memories of human life is in vain. Only the radiators still cling to the walls, like big frightened beasts, but otherwise everything that could burn has vanished. There is no wind today but when the wind is high it bangs those radiators and the whole deathly ex-suburb echoes with a weird hammering. Now and again it happens that a radiator suddenly comes loose and falls down and kills someone who is groping around for coal in the innards of the ruin.

Looking for coal, that is one of the reasons why people step off the train at Landwehr. With a lost

Silesia in mind, with the prospect of losing the Saar and with a Ruhr whose fate is by no means uncontested, sarcastic Germans refer to the ruins as Germany's only coalmines.

But she in whose company I look for a house that does not exist is not so sarcastic. She is a half-Jewish German who by making herself as invisible as possible managed to survive the terror and the war. She was in Spain until Franco's victory made it impossible for her to stay there and then she came back to Germany. She lived near Landwehr until the house was blown to pieces by English bombs. She is a vigorously bitter woman who lost all her possessions in the bombing of Hamburg and who had already lost her faith and hope in the bombing of Guernica.

We wander around in this endless shambles of a graveyard where it is quite hopeless to find one's way: there is nothing to distinguish one annihilated block from another. On the occasional surviving wall there may hang a derisive-looking plate with a street name; of an entire tenement there may be nothing left but the main doorway crowned with a meaningless number. Signboards from old greengrocers' and butchers' shops which were buried under the wreckage stick up out of the rubble like inscriptions on gravestones, but in a building near by a light suddenly sparkles out from a cellar.

We have reached a district whose luck it was to come through the destruction with its cellars intact. The buildings have collapsed but the cellar roofs have held and now they give shelter to hundreds of bombed families. Through the small windows we see the small rooms with bare cement walls, a stove, a bed, a table, and at best a chair. Children play with stones on the floor, a pot stands on the stove. In the ruin above, white children's clothes flutter on a washing-line stretched between a twisted water-pipe and a fallen iron girder. The smoke from the stoves finds its way out through the cracks in disintegrating walls. Empty prams wait outside the cellar windows.

A dentist and a few grocers have set up shop at the bottom of a ruin. Wherever a scrap of earth is available red cabbages are cultivated.

'The Germans are a capable people at any rate,' my guide says and falls silent.

At any rate. It sounds as if she is sorry.

Farther down the street an English lorry stands, its engine idling. Some English soldiers have got out and are clowning for the benefit of a group of small children.

'The English are nice to children at any rate.'

It sounds as if she is sorry about that too.

But when I try to tell her that I am sorry about the loss of her home she is one of the very few who say: 'It began in Coventry.'

The line sounds almost too classic to be genuine but in her case it is genuine. She knows all about what has happened in the war and yet, or perhaps because of that, her case is so tragic.

For there is in Germany a large group of honest anti-fascists who are more disappointed, homeless and defeated than the Nazi fellow-travellers can ever be: disappointed because the liberation did not turn out to be as radical as they had thought it would be; homeless because they did not want to associate themselves either with the overall German dissatisfaction, among whose ingredients they thought they could detect far too much hidden Nazism, or with the politics of the Allies, whose compliance in the face of the former Nazis they regard with dismay; and, finally, defeated because they doubt whether as Germans they can hold shares in the final victory of the Allies while at the same time they are equally unconvinced that as anti-Nazis they can be partners in the German defeat. They have condemned themselves to complete passivity because activity means co-operation with the dubious elements which in the course of twelve years of oppression they have learned to hate.

These people are Germany's most beautiful ruins, but for the present as uninhabitable as the collapsed masses of ruined dwellings between Hasselbrook and Landwehr, which smell acrid and bitter from quenched fires in the wet autumn twilight.

Bombed Cemetery

On a bridge in Hamburg there is a man standing selling a little gadget: fastened to an ordinary knife, it is meant to give a more economical method of peeling potatoes. He puts on such a show when he demonstrates how using this new invention the potato-peel can be as thin as anyone could want, that all of us, who have been standing at the railing watching how heavy black barges loaded with rubble are poled up the canal, turn away and gather round him. No one is likely to satisfy his hunger by joking about it, even in Hamburg, but to be able to laugh at it provides an entertaining form of forgetfulness which the people of this hungry land are seldom willing to forgo.

The man on the bridge holds up his solitary little demonstration-potato in the autumn sun and announces that it's a devil of a job peeling potatoes as big as those allowed by the rations . . . A fishmonger near by shows the same kind of humour when he puts up a huge, indignant notice in his empty shop-window: 'Imagine raising the fish rations now when we're *so* short of wrapping-paper.' He gets the laughers on his side, if not the buyers, yet.

But at one end of the bridge there is a tram-stop. A

27

little old woman with a big sack of potatoes has just mounted the platform when the tram sets off. The sack tips over, the string loosens, the old lady screams as the tram rolls by us and the potatoes begin to drum on the roadway. A violent stir is felt among those crowded about the street-seller and when the tram has passed he is standing almost alone by the railing while his audience scuffle over the potatoes among hooting English army cars and Volkswagens in war-paint. Schoolchildren fill their satchels, workers stuff their pockets full, housewifes open their handbags for Germany's most sought-after fruit, and two minutes later, laughing and eager to buy, they have surrounded the seller of the device intended to procure Germany's thinnest potato-peel – after one of those abrupt switches from fury to friendliness which make the people of Hamburg so exciting and so risky to mix with.

But why does Fräulein S. not laugh? As I leave the bridge with her I ask her right out why she did not laugh, but instead of answering she says bitterly: 'That's Germany today – risk your life for a potato.'

But in fact not laughing at the need on the streets of Hamburg is only what could be expected of Fräulein S. Since the collapse of Germany she has been working in a labour office in Hamburg but before that she had a fishmonger's shop that was burnt up in the celluloid bombing in 1943. Now she spends two hours each day inspecting a district of ruins, checking that those capable of work are at work, and seeing to it that those who cannot look after themselves are cared for. The person who introduced me to Fräulein S. confided in me that she is one of the many Germans

28

who are Nazis without knowing it and who would be mortally offended if anyone dared to suggest that her views were similar to those of the Nazis. Fräulein S. is said to be very bitter but at the same time grateful for a job that gives her the chance of keeping her bitterness on the boil. She is undoubtedly an energetic and go-ahead person, but she is also a confirmation of the idea held by many, though of course not all, anti-Nazis: that dubious opinions are the price of energy in today's Germany.

It is tempting to talk politics with someone who does not realize that one knows something about them, especially if that someone is German and is supposed to have Nazi sympathies without being aware of the fact. Which party does such a person vote for? (Local elections have just been held in Hamburg.)

Fräulein S. answers without a moment's hesitation. For her there was only one party, 'the Social Democrats of course', but on further questioning – 'why exactly them?' – she can give no more rational explanation than the majority of SDP voters. In fact like most Germans of her way of thinking Fräulein S. chose her party by process of elimination: the Christian Democrats are eliminated because one is not religious, the Communists will not do because one is afraid of the Russians, the Liberals are too few to play a significant role, the Conservatives are too unknown, so that leaves the SDP if one is going to vote – and one does vote, despite the fact that one says it cannot matter who wins an election in a country that is still occupied.

We come out into a wide ruined square where a tall

solitary lift-shaft has been forgotten by the bombs. A few workers are pulling a little cart loaded with stone and scrap and when they come to the street a woman with a red flag steps out quite pointlessly and stops the traffic which is not there.

'You see, Mr D.,' says the frost-bitten woman who is with me and she takes my arm, 'we Germans think it is high time the Allies stopped punishing us. Whatever people can say about us Germans and what our soldiers have done in other countries, we have not deserved the punishment we are now getting.'

'Punishment?' I wonder. 'Why do you think it's a punishment that things here are as they are?'

'Because things have got worse instead of better. We feel we are sinking and that we still have a long way to go to reach the bottom.'

And then she tells me the popular and unfortunately too well confirmed story of the English captain who when asked why the English would not let Hamburg's railway stations be rebuilt replied: 'Why should we help you Germans to get on your feet in three years when it could just as well take thirty?'

Meanwhile we have reached a huge, gloomy, scarred building that looks like a delapidated city school but is Hamburg's former Gestapo prison. The stairways and the washrooms on the landings are discreetly silent about what was happening here only a year ago. We grope along a pitch-black corridor full of embarrassing smells. Suddenly Fräulein S. knocks on a tall iron-door and we step into one of the communal cells, a big bare room with a cement floor and a window that has been almost entirely bricked-up. A solitary bulb hangs from the ceiling and shines unmercifully on three air-raid-shelter beds, a stove reeking with sour wood, a small woman with a chalk-white face stirring a pot on the stove, a small boy lying on a bed staring up apathetically at the light.

Fräulein S. tells a lie and says we are looking for a family called Müller. The woman has scarcely noticed that we have come in. Without looking up from the pot she says that Hans cannot go out today because he has no shoes.

'How many of you live here?' Fräulein S. asks and steps forward to look in the pot.

'Nine,' says the tired woman, 'eight children and myself. Deported from Bavaria. Lived here since July. This week we were lucky and got wood. Last week we were lucky and got potatoes.'

'How do you manage then?'

'Like this,' says the woman, lifting the ladle from the pot and gesturing hopelessly round the cell. Then she begins stirring again. The smoke stings our eyes. The boy lies still and quiet as death on the bed, staring up at the ceiling. The woman does not notice when we leave.

The entire prison is full of families who were evacuated from Hamburg to Bavaria in 1943 and then expelled by the Bavarian government in the summer of 1946. I think I detect a melancholy satisfaction in Fräulein S.'s voice when we return to the open air.

'The English could still have helped us. They had the chance to show what democracy is but they didn't take it. You see, Mr D., it would have been another matter if we Germans had been living a life of abundance and luxury in the Hitler years, but we were poor, Mr D. And the fact is we have lost everything: homes, families, possessions. And how do you think we suffered during the raids! Do we need to be punished more – haven't we been punished enough already?'

We visit a cellar beneath a shoemaker's workshop where three people and an infant live in a foul-smelling windowless room. I recall what a wise German said about the often lamented absence of guilt feelings in the civilian population of Germany (it was slightly different in the case of the soldiers).

'Perhaps we know that it began in Coventry but we were not there. We were there in Hamburg, and it was in Berlin and Hannover and Essen we went through three years of mortal fear day after day. This lack of guilt should be regretted, it need not be understood, but one ought to keep in mind that one's own sufferings make it more difficult to understand other people's sufferings.'

Fräulein S. and I end the day in a former school lavatory in Altona. The school is in fragments but in the lavatory in the playground there lives a Sudeten-German family with three children. The man searches for wire in the ruins and earns a living by selling the ornaments he makes with the wire. It looks surprisingly neat in this urinal and the man is touchingly happy about having at last got his own home, and he tells us without any false sympathy how pleased he was when he eventually managed to persuade the 'tenant' who lived here before him to move out. At that time the urinal was still a urinal and this previous 'tenant' gave up when in the course of a short period TB robbed him of his mother, his father, his wife and his daughter in the school lavatory in Altona.

Before we return to the centre of Hamburg Fräulein S. takes me to a street that runs past a Jewish cemetery. The cemetery has been bombed, the gravestones are broken off and sooty. In the background there is a mutilated church with black walls. A few people in mourning kneel before fresh dark mounds of earth.

Then Fräulein S. says: 'This is Germany, Mr D., a bombed cemetery. When I pass this way I always stop for a little and look.'

It is a devotional moment or two I witness here in this little street in Altona, a brief minute of happiness for someone who thanks God because she is allowed to live in hell.

But when I discreetly turn away to leave her alone with her bitter happiness I read on a huge banner stretched across the wall of a ruin a giant advertisement for *The Merry Widow*. Widow, yes – but merry?

Poor Man's Cake

Deep within a neglected park on the outskirts of Hamburg there lives an ageing liberal lawyer together with a writer of picaresque novels. The park is in an area of Hamburg where the streets have no other lighting than the headlamps of English vehicles as they prowl past. In the darkness you bump against invisible arms or hear invisible words in passing and with a shiver you remind yourself of the advice given by experienced correspondents – not to venture out on the dark streets of Hamburg without the company of a revolver. The park is a wilder place than it seems in daylight, but at last you reach a safe flight of steps, you ring the bell and are admitted to a large better-class hallway with an umbrella-stand and a Silesian maid. In the lounge the ornamental time-piece, the metres of gold-edged morocco-bound volumes in the bookshelves, the dense carpet, the chandelier, the leather armchairs – none of this gives one hint of the bombing and the desperate housing shortage. And what about the lawyer and the writer?

The most cherished slogan of current middle-class election propaganda is the claim that the defeat has abolished classes in Germany. The labour parties are reproved for using a mere fiction as a cudgel in their fight against bourgeois resistance. In fact it was no coincidence that during the election in the autumn of 1946 the battle-cries of class warfare echoed with particular bitterness. The thesis of a classless Germany involved a cynical exaggeration. After the collapse, class frontiers have been sharpened rather than blurred. The bourgeois ideologists confuse poverty and classlessness when they assert that by and large all Germans are financially in the same desperate straits. In one way it is true that most Germans are poor and that many who used to be well-heeled are now down-at-heel, but in Germany there is a difference between the least poor and the most poor which is greater than the difference between those who own much and those who own nothing in a more or less normally endowed society.

While the most poor live in the cellars of ruins, in bunkers or in one-time prison cells, and the middling poor crowd together in the abandoned tenements one family to a room, the least poor live in their old villas (like the liberal lawyer and the writer) or in the town's most spacious apartments, where not even the middling poor can afford to live. The lawyer is of course right when he says that the English bombs crossed the frontiers of class, even if, as was natural, the less densely populated residential areas came off more lightly than the packed tenements. But in defence of the class struggle one ought to add that the bank accounts were not bombed. Admittedly, bank accounts are blocked in such a way that it is impossible to draw more than 120 marks per month, a modest sum when you think that that is precisely the price of half a kilo of butter on the black market. Here too for the sake of justice one ought to add that the average wage can amount to 120 marks per month, and that money hoarded at home for safety quite simply escapes the eye of authority.

And this leads to the most absurd, incredible and unfair consequences. A common judgement in the denazification trials is that the accused, if he has been active as a Nazi, is deprived of his apartment, which is then allocated to someone who has suffered political oppression. The gesture is fine, but alas often meaningless, because economically anyone who has suffered political persecution finds himself somewhere between the middling poor and the most poor and simply cannot pay the rent for a large ex-Nazi apartment, which is now taken over instead by people with money, and that means people who earned money under the aegis of Nazism.

The liberal lawyer and his friend the writer of picaresque novels have never been Nazis. Before 1933 the lawyer belonged to the old Liberal Party and the writer is one of the very few best-selling authors who during the Hitler years preferred to live off their money rather than write. As we drink tea without sugar and eat a cake which beneath its layer of carefully counterfeited cream turns out to be the usual bad German *ersatz* bread, the lawyer reveals, under his silver-haired surface of resignation, a passionate sense of disillusion which is quite rare among the bitter indifference so common in Germany and which in normal countries would be attributed to youthful hysteria. It seems to be a part of good German post-war breeding in certain middle-class circles that not-so-young gentlemen relate how they have spent the last twelve years with one foot in the concentration camp, a habit to be found also in the worst circles, those of the still-to-be-denazified. What is even rarer is to hear those words expressed with genuine rather than false pathos, but this master of fragile resignation who leans over the equally fragile Meissen porcelain has developed the art to a nicety.

'We greeted the Englishmen as liberators, but they can't have realized that. We were willing to do everything, to get not the old Germany but a new democracy on to its feet. But we weren't allowed to. And now we are disappointed in the English because we have a definite impression that they are sabotaging the process of renewal, and indifferent to what is happening because they are stronger than we are.'

'We' – that can mean the Liberal Party, which in North Germany is rather small but has a good reputation on account of its anti-Nazi attitude, but which in South Germany is large and suspect for there we can hear it said 'Think Liberal, act Socialist and feel German.' But 'We' can mean much else. 'We' can be those middle-class German intellectuals who were at heart anti-Nazi but never had to suffer for this and perhaps never wanted to suffer for it, who never voluntarily went against the grain and are now bearing a kind of anti-Nazi *jalousie de métier* against the legitimated anti-Nazis, those who were politically persecuted. Having two consciences in one's breast, one good and one bad, promotes neither ideological nor psychological clarity. Disappointement and conscious disillusionment are without doubt the simplest way out for such a dilemma of the soul.

The author is more flexible by constitution and laughingly tells us that the programmes of the different parties are still so obscurely couched that people will turn up at the wrong election meeting and only at the exit, even if then, notice that they have visited the Social Democrats instead of the Christian Democrats or the Liberal Democrats instead of the Conservatives. He himself illustrates the ideological confusion in an apt and amusing way. He claims to have been born an anti-Nazi but yet he has voted for the CDU, the party which calls itself Christian and is said to have gathered pretty well all of the former Nazis under its cross in the hope of avoiding a planned economy and the loss of their money. But in order to salve his conscience he has persuaded his sister, who is Conservative but lacks money, to stand in for him and vote for the Social Democrats.

The habit of writing optimistic novels persists, although it is fifteen years since the last one. He assures us on his honour that at the most a mere one per cent of the German 'quality' were Nazis, whereupon the lawyer drily laments the lack of 'quality' in Germany. The latter goes on to accuse the English: he says that through a deliberate policy of starvation they have demoralized the population to just as great an extent as the Nazis did, they have 'made bad people worse and good people uncertain', with the consequence that they are driven into the arms of whatever suspect movement you can name, so long as it undertakes to solve their immediate material problems.

It is, of course, a bitter truth that hunger is unamenable to any form of idealism. The work of ideological reconstruction in Germany today meets the strongest opposition not in those who are consciously reactionary but in the indifferent masses who are letting questions of political persuasion wait until they have been fed. Allowing for this, the most polished election propaganda is content to promise, after victory at the polls, not peace and freedom, but a proper larder, proof against rats and thieves, and Germany's best-known loaf is the one that appeared, with a sharp bread-knife, on the Communist posters in the autumn of 1946. One rainy day in October when General Koenig, the liberator of Paris, stepped out under the bullet-riddled canopy of Hamburg's Central Station, both he and the nervous British guards, officers with white sleeve-covers up to their elbows and plenty of red both on their cheeks and on their parade uniforms – all were observed by dense rows of the unemployed of Hamburg. When the long cortège of cars drew away with angry tootings the young German police lads were surrounded by people scornfully shouting 'What did he bring? Chocolate? Or bread?' And the representatives of the powers of law and order blushed beneath their leather helmets.

To blush – that, until further notice, is all that the parties can do when the masses demand some end to their material difficulties. But there are more becoming and less becoming ways of blushing. One of the less becoming is the middle-class insistence on the dissolution of the class society, though at heart one knows perfectly well that they don't mean it. The cake of bad German bread offered by the lawyer and the author is in fact a symbolic cake, a liberal cake whose imitation cream is intended to camouflage all too bitter facts. It is without doubt a cake for the least poor. The most poor do not eat bread that way.

This symbolic cake implies one of the reasons why the labour parties are evolving their strategies along the lines of class struggle and why certain groups in the trade union movement have the foresight to expect hitherto unseen social conflicts when the occupying powers eventually give Germany a free rein. To find more concrete evidence you can take a ride on one of Hamburg's underground trains, where you can travel second class along with relatively well-dressed and relatively well-maintained citizens, and third class along with ragged citizens whose faces are white as chalk or paper, faces which look as if they could never blush, faces which, you might think, would not even bleed if they were cut. These, the whitest faces in Germany, most definitely do not belong to the class of the least poor.

The Art of Sinking

Sink a little! Try to sink a little! When it comes to the art of sinking then there are worse and better artists. In Germany there are bad practitioners who keep themselves alive only by the thought that since they have so little to live for they have even less to die for. But there are surprisingly many who are willing to accept anything merely to survive.

On Sundays outside the Zoo Station in Berlin a ragged and blind old man sits playing shrill psalm-tunes on a little portable organ. He sits bare-headed in the cold and listens sorrowfully down in the direction of his shabby cap on the pavement, but the German coins make a faint dull clink and only rarely do they fall in the caps of the blind. It would of course be a little better for him if he did not play the organ and above all if he did not play psalms. On weekday afternoons when the people of Berlin draw past with their small creaking hand-carts after yet another day of hunting for potatoes or firewood in the less harrowed suburbs the blind man has exchanged his harmonium for a barrel-organ, and the coins drop more frequently, but on Sunday he insists with quite uneconomic idealism on using his squeaky harmonium. On Sundays he cannot accept his hurdy-gurdy. He still has a little bit further to sink.

But in the stations it is possible to meet people who have passed most of the stages. The big German railway stations, once the scene for mannequin shows and adventures, contain between their scarred walls and beneath their cracked roofs a high percentage of the sum of hopelessness. In rainy weather the stranger is always surprised to see and hear the rain pattering down through the waiting-room roof and forming lakes on the floor between the benches. It seems like a tiny revolution in this disciplined chaos. At night the stranger will start as he stumbles against refugees in the concrete tunnels, refugees from the east or from the south, lying stretched out on the naked floor along the naked walls and either sleeping heavily or sitting crouched among their poor bundles and waiting all too wide awake for a train that will take them to a new station, just as hopeless as this one.

The underground stations in the big cities have come through in better shape. They are rundown but unscathed. Berlin's *Untergrundbahnstationen* smell of wetness and poverty, but the trains run promptly as in peacetime. One does not turn to stare at the foreign soldiers walking the platforms with well-dressed but badly painted German girls who are already speaking perfectly whiny American or quick conciliatory English. Many of these girls stand leaning against the sides of the train-doors trying to catch as many eyes as possible with their provocative glances and telling their English soldier that the people here have no sense; others prop up their drunk American friend and make eyes that say: 'What can a poor girl do?'

The smoke from their Allied cigarettes blends inside the compartments with the smoke of the German cigarettes, which tastes sour and stifling, and gives the underground trains their persistent smell of dirt and destitution. But when the underground trains come up into the sharp light of day these girls too have faces with the shadows of hunger. And it happens – rarely, no doubt, but it does happen – that someone says: 'That's what the future of Germany looks like! A drunk pimply American and a whore of a German girl!'

It happens rarely because sheer necessity wears down the habit of moralizing on behalf of others. It is not true to claim, as a well-fed army chaplain from California said over his steak on the Northern Express, that Germany is a country quite without morality. It is just that in this country of privation morality has acquired quite a new dimension, whose very existence unaccustomed eyes simply do not notice. This new morality postulates that there are conditions in which it is not immoral to steal since in these circumstances theft means not depriving someone of his property but a more just distribution of available goods; likewise black-marketing and prostitution are not immoral when they have become the only means of survival. This does not of course mean that everyone steals, that everyone deals on the black-market or goes in for prostitution, but it does mean that even among certain youthful church groups people consider that for the sake of endurance it is from a moral point of view more reprehensible to starve or let your family starve than to do something which in a normal sense is forbidden. The necessary crime is regarded with more tolerance in Germany

45

than anywhere else; that is one aspect of what the Allied chaplain calls lack of morality. Sinking is more readily forgiven than going under.

One afternoon as darkness is falling and when there is a power cut in Berlin I met a little Polish school-teacher in the twilight of a station where the trains to Potsdam rattle past. She has a boy of seven who is taking a childish interest in the remains of a two-year-old train crash out at the edge of the sidings. Passenger coaches with crushed skulls lie tumbled and broken along the side of the rails, a burnt out bogie-car has hurtled into the rusty skeleton of a disintegrated sleeping-car, two goods wagons stand defiantly at cross-purposes, and dead limbs of undercarriages stick up out of the fragments.

By the side of the track all the way into Berlin there are old rusty train wrecks. At each station the platforms are black with people. Crowds with ruck-sacks, bundles of brushwood, cabbage-heads in tattered paper, and little carts, all rush in through the doors and all the time between two stations there is someone or other wailing in pain. Two women screech unceasingly over a trifle. Trampled dogs whimper but on a bench sit two silent Russian officers surrounded by a little wall of frightened respect.

In short sentences constantly broken off by the crush at new stations or by curses from people whose rucksacks are too big I slowly find out what it feels like to live in great loneliness in Berlin. The Polish teacher lost her husband in Auschwitz and then she lost two children on the road from the Polish border to Berlin in the big panic in 1945, and the seven-year-old boy is all she has left. Yet she has a calm face

46

when the lights come on, and when I ask her what she busies herself with she whispers with a laugh in my ear: '*Geschäft*!' At one time she read Hamsum and Strindberg in a little Polish village, but '*jetzt ist alles vorbei*'.

What, though, does she mean by '*Geschäft*?' We talk for a little about longing, since everyone who is forced to remain in Germany longs to be where they are not, unless they are too old to be able to long, or unless they have the desperate courage to believe they have a mission. The Polish teacher longs for Sweden or Norway. She has a picture at home that helps her with her longing. It shows a Norwegian fjord – or the Danube at Siebenbrügen. Would I come home and say which, to save her from longing in the wrong direction?

From the underground station we have many dark streets to negotiate. There has just been an election and the big posters are still hanging on the walls of the ruins. The Social Democrats: 'Where there is fear there is no freedom; without freedom there is no democracy.' The Communists: 'Youth belongs to us.' The Christian Democrats: 'Christianity, Socialism, Democracy.' The CDU is a chameleon who won in Hamburg thanks to crude anti-Marxist propaganda and tried to win in Berlin through an equally diligent use of the word 'socialism'.

'But what does "*Geschäft*" in fact mean?'

If whispered it means the black market, if said out loud it means business in general. She has a two-room flat by itself at the top of a tenement whose roof has been blasted off. People are already standing waiting on the stairs. Someone who wants to get rid of

47

a clock. Someone else who has suddenly realized that he needs an oriental carpet. An old lady, fine as china, who would rather have something to eat instead of her old solid silver service. The door-bell rings all evening and the big room is full of people eagerly muttering about porcelain, clocks, furs, carpets and incredible sums of money. I sit in a small inner room and try to chat with the silent boy who is seven but whose eyes are at least ten years older. The picture shows a completely anonymous landscape. I drink tea with rare white sugar. In a pause the teacher comes in and says she doesn't like all this.

'Once I was so shy I'd hardly open my mouth. Now I spend my days travelling round trying to sniff out people who have gold and silver. You mustn't think I like it. But one has to live, here too. And if you want to live you have to get used to anything.'

Yes, one must live, and of course one must get used to anything. Her companion, a newly returned soldier, comes in and keeps me company for a time. He was in Italy and has a damaged forehead as a memento of the first Allied landing on Sicily and a grenade-splinter in his breast as a souvenir of the siege of Monte Cassino. If he is reproved for being a black-marketeer he says: 'I have an allowance of forty-five marks a month. That's enough for seven cigarettes.'

When asked if he was a Nazi he replies that he spent seven years in the war and that he takes that to be enough of an answer. When asked if he has voted he says he has, but it won't do any good. And which party? The Christian Democrats? No, he is not religious. The Communists? No, he has friends who were POWs in Russian camps. That leaves the Social

Democrats, because they mean least to him.

But he carries memories not only from Nettuno and Monte Cassino, but also from a Berlin that was once a friendly place. He is able to tell jokes. He tells me the one about the four occupiers of Berlin who rule over a pond and each has his own goldfish. The Russian catches his goldfish and eats it up. The Frenchman catches his and throws it away after pulling off the beautiful fins. The American stuffs his and sends it home to the USA as a souvenir. The Englishman behaves most strangely of all: he catches his fish, holds it in his hand and caresses it to death.

This freezing, starving, surreptitiously bargaining, dirty and immoral Berlin can still tell funny stories, can still be friendly enough to ask lonely strangers home to tea, still has such people as this Polish teacher and this soldier, who are certainly living unlawfully but who serve, paradoxically enough, as points of light in a great darkness, since they have sufficient courage to sink with their eyes open.

But as I take the oddly-smelling underground home in the evening there is a small drunk English soldier-boy sitting between two dissipated blondes whose rigid smiles look as if they belonged to the wrong faces. He caresses both of them but then when he leaves the train alone the smiles quickly drop from the faces, and the two girls set up a raw, humourless wrangle that lasts for over three stations and the air tingles with hysteria. Nothing could be less like goldfish than those two.

The Unwelcome

Nowadays goods trains generally have priority on German railways. The same people who bitterly claim that Germans have been degraded to a third-class people when the occupying powers have taken season tickets for several rows in the city theatre, sit in the ice-cold compartments of the shabby passenger trains and interpret the new train system symbolically. One must certainly learn to wait: certain kinds of goods train are considered more important than several fully loaded freezing passenger trains bulging with people and their newly filled or still empty potato-sacks.

But there are goods trains and goods trains. There are goods trains that are considered to be so insignificant that they are shunted into side-tracks at the junctions, forgotten or neglected and left to stand there for days on end until they are sent on. These trains usually arrive unannounced out of the night and are treated by dispatchers and authorities with the appropriate sort of reluctance that always meets the uninvited. In spite of that, the unwelcome goods trains continue, with embarrassing persistence, to reveal themselves like ghost-ships at the stations, and the railway staff continue to send them on when the

51

line at some point is by chance open.

One can well understand this reluctance and hesitation on the part of the railway officials. The uninvited goods trains are hardly models of their kind; they are not even typical examples of German post-war rolling-stock. They consist of wagons which in normal times would go to the scrap-heap, but which are now coupled together and supplied with small informative signs saying: 'Not watertight. Unsuitable for the transport of perishable goods.' This means that the rain comes in through the roof and that the wagon can therefore be used only for the transport of goods which do not rust and in general will not suffer from being soaked through or which quite simply are thought to be so worthless that it would not matter if they really did come to harm – in other words, things not worth the effort of stealing and scarcely deserving the use of a goods train claiming respect and priority when its approach is signalled down the line.

In a cold grey downpour such a train is standing in a marshalling yard in Essen. It consists of nineteen wagons and has spent the whole week parked here in the rain. The engine was uncoupled, and the interest which usually greets the arrival of useful-looking goods trains has not been forthcoming in this case. And yet this abandoned, famished goods train contains something which ought to be of great interest to the city of Essen: two hundred citizens of Essen who have been evacuees in Bavaria since the first Allied blanket-bombing spread over the Ruhr and who have now returned in this train to their home city or rather to the station of their home city because they are not allowed to come further.

All Germans know that most of the larger German cities are subject to *Zuzugsverbot*, which means that travel within Germany is forbidden to the extent that while one is permitted to walk about among the ruins of any German city one chooses, it is none the less forbidden to look for work, to eat or to live there. The Bavarian authorities know that too, but their knowledge did not prevent them from evicting, at five days' notice, the non-Bavarian evacuees who had been assigned to the unscathed Bavarian villages. The non-watertight goods trains are put together in Bavarian stations, the non-Bavarians are stuffed into the wagons, whose sole amenities consist of floor, roof and walls, and as soon as the line is clear the trains are sent off towards the north-west.

Fourteen days later a train reaches its destination, and its destination first does not know about its arrival, and then does not want to know. During the fourteen days in which the train was on its way its passengers were not furnished with any official possibility of being fed, but their home city shows a little goodwill in offering a plate of thin soup per day in a small shed at the side of the tracks.

It is embarrassing and highly unpleasant coming to such a place and feeling quite helpless. The main station-building vanished several years ago and twisted rails coil like snakes beyond the one track that has been put in order, and there the lonely goods train stands. The cracked platform has been made muddy by the endless rain. Some of the passengers wander up and down outside the wagons, whose doors are half open to the grey day. I have come here with a young medical officer whose painful duty it is

53

to state that the inhabitants of the train are in a poor state of health and to tell them that unfortunately the city authorities can do nothing about their state of health.

His arrival however rouses vain hopes in the starving passengers. An old woman leans out over a rusty stove-pipe and calls us. It turns out she has a two-year-old granddaughter lying on a little bed in there in the darkness. Apart from when she coughs, the girl lies quite still. The poverty of the goods wagon: a ragged bed along one wall, a pile of potatoes tipped into a corner (the only provisions during this journey without a destination), a small heap of dirty straw in another corner, where three people sleep, and all muffled in the calm blue smoke from the ramshackle stove, which was rescued from one of Essen's ruins. Here two families live, six people in all. There were eight of them to start with, but two hopped off somewhere along the way and never came back. Dr W. can of course lift the girl up and say how she is, he can carry her over to the light coming from the open flap of the stove and declare that immediate hospital treatment is needed urgently, but then he must also explain how there are no vacant places in the hospitals and how the city's administrative bureaucracy is as usual considerably more slow-moving than death.

When the grandmother asks the young doctor to do something he must therefore first clench his teeth and swallow and say that he has come here not to help them but to show a Swedish journalist 'how nicely we travel in German trains these days'. A young boy in a shabby naval uniform, lying on his back in the straw, laughs hilariously at the joke.

Rumours of our arrival have in the meantime spread through the whole train, and children and old people are waiting impatiently in the rain and cascading us with questions. Someone has heard that the train is going to be put back on the line and sent off somewhere and not even the engine-driver has the least idea where the train is to go this time. Someone else earnestly begs the doctor to arrange it so that the train can be immediately driven out into the country-side, where the passengers can themselves find some way of living.

'With the farmers,' someone hisses indignantly. 'We've had enough of our farmers!'

Someone else has a sick mother lying in the straw, starved and coughing – but what is the good of visiting her when all one can offer is consolation instead of medicine? A sympathetic young family hand down a little baby through the wagon opening and ask me to hold him for a moment. He is a small blue one-year-old whose eyes are inflamed by the draughts in the wagon; his parents are simultaneously proud and anxious. The husband insists on letting me know that all the travellers on this train know where the responsibility lies, ultimately it is Hitler and no one else who is to blame, but the authorities down in Bavaria, which is the least affected part of the whole nation, could have behaved in a less inconsiderate manner, and at least they could have warned the Essen authorities that they could expect a train.

'Our lords and masters may be in charge,' says a lively old lady from the darkness inside the wagon, 'but it's always us who get stuck in the middle.'

On the whole spirits are quite high in spite of the

hardships. The knowledge that none of them needs to suffer alone has generated a kind of communal wellbeing that spills over into black humour. The sides of the wagons are covered with chalked grafitti: the old Anschluss slogan, *'Heim ins Reich'* now in an ironic context, or *'Wir danken dem Herrn Högner für die freie Fahrt'* – we thank Herr Högner (Bavaria's Social Democrat Minister-President) for the free journey – or a drawing of an ox-load with the inscription 'Bavarian farmers can now carry their own dung.' And everywhere that infamous notice about the wagons' liability to let the rain in. The doctor strikes it with an angry glove.

'No longer suitable for goods. Only for people.'

And more bitterly: 'Just think, fellow-countrymen evicting fellow-countrymen. Germans against Germans. The worst of all.'

The very fact that it is Germans who are responsible for having dispatched this train seems to cause him more distress than the condition of the train and its occupants. The young doctor is a Conservative anti-fascist who at a pinch can regard even Nazism from the point of view of national necessity. When he talks about the occupation of Norway, where he was sent as an army doctor just after passing his exams, he tells me about wonderful ski trips in the moonlight on the Norwegian mountains near where he was stationed. Hearing him speak like this one would think the Germans occupied Norway for the sake of winter sports. And yet it is hard to avoid feeling that Dr W. is in his way a decent person.

Now at any rate he is sufficiently well bred and sufficiently honest to accept and even co-operate loyally with the Allied authorities in the cleaning up of

Essen. But for him, as for many other young people from the better-off classes who were nourished not on Nazism but on an idealistic nationalism which involves a respectable kind of ruthlessness in victory and loyal dignity in defeat, the experience of German ruthlessness towards Germans comes as a terrible shock.

It is possible that in this respect the country is now finding itself in a situation unique for Germany: the conflicts between the large interest-groups within the population are so acute that to a certain extent they deprive the reactionary powers which exist in the people's consciousness of an operational base from which they can conduct effective neo-nationalist propaganda. The passengers on this train hate Bavarian farmers and Bavarians in general, and the relatively prosperous Bavaria looks with mild contempt on the hysteria rampant in the rest of Germany. City people accuse country people of letting food land up on the black market, while country people in turn maintain that city people rove about the countryside like plunderers. The refugees from the east speak bitterly about the Russians and the Poles, but are themselves regarded as intruders and end up living in a state of war with the people of the west. The oppressive atmosphere in the west is criss-crossed by rancorous feelings which are as yet not explicit enough to cause more than isolated explosions of violence.

A good many of the people on the train have been into town and found their old apartments taken over by strangers. Now they are sitting in the straw nursing their bitterness, but on the platform two old ladies are arguing about how Hitler really can be alive, as the rumours in the Western Zone have it.

'*Der Schweinehund*,' says the elder and more ragged of the two and makes a cutting gesture across her throat. 'If only we had him here!'

In the meantime some members of the Swedish Red Cross have arrived with dried milk for those children on the train who are under four. We search through the train, followed by a begging crowd who are clearly older but who are still hoping for something. Someone opens a closed door on one of the wagons and a ragged white-haired patriarch appears from the darkness.

'No, no children here,' he stammers, 'only my wife and myself. We're nearly eighty. We live here. It's our fate. *So ist unser los.*'

And in a dignified manner he closes the door. But in another wagon there is a girl in a wheelchair in a state of shock. The uniform seen in passing must have wakened some terrible memory in her, for she breaks out in a scream, a dreadful shrill cry that suddenly cracks and gives way to a dog-like whining. The rain is pouring down, and the barefoot boys are running about silently on the platform. The smoke from the stove-pipes protruding from the doors spreads its veil slowly out over the abandoned marshalling yard. All the hopelessness of the Ruhr is lying like a grey cloud of leaden wet coldness over our heads; anyone coming to this for the first time would find it hard not to scream. Someone lifts down the hysterical girl's wheelchair and begins to wheel it round on the platform. Round and round in the rain and mud.

The Rivals

It is convenient but not necessarily helpful to regard Germany as a patient, Europe's 'sick man', in desperate need of injections of anti-Nazi serum. There is no doubt that in one way or another Germany ought to be cleansed of Nazism, but what is doubtful in this connection is that the patient theory presupposes a mystical unity which simply does not exist in Germany today. It is just not the case that the German people are thus divided into two blocs: a small anti-Nazi victory monument of gravestone dimensions, and a huge Nazi memorial of vast proportions ready to tip over at the least puff of opposition and bury all the little barricades of freedom under its threatening weight of marble.

Anyone who has spent some time with Germans from different levels of society soon discovers that what appeared upon a brief acquaintance with current German thinking as an unbroken unity is in fact a mesh of diagonal, vertical and horizontal cracks. What was assumed to be unshakeable unity is only a superficial agreement on certain elementary opinions: all Germans think that the seven million POWs should come home and that those who come home should weigh more – quite physically – than those Germans who return from Russian arsenals and French mines. All Germans agree that the zone boundaries should be abolished and that the dismantling of industrial plant, if it is really necessary, should not mean for example that expensive machine-parts confiscated by the Russians are left to lie rusting away on barges in Hamburg's docks. Further, all Germans in the Western Zone agree, albeit on the basis of differing premisses, that the huge consignments of refugees from the east to the west are a form of invisible pressure exerted by the Russians on the Allies; by pumping the Allied zones full of destitute people the Russians would be able to create quickly a situation of *Verelendigung* which at a given moment of maximum stress must give vent to an explosion of a kind devastating for the Western occupying powers.

Opinions with regard to the Allies are unanimous only in the sense that a certain feeling of restriction is common to all Germans. Still, it is felt even in strongly reactionary circles that there is no objective basis for any sort of resistance, including the passive sort. In reality the Germans regard themselves as occupied in a different way, for instance, from how the French regarded themselves as occupied: one finds no public contempt for the occupying power, hardly even for the occupier's girl-friends, and the only kind of democratic education which the Allies have so far attempted – the efforts made by the Americans to turn German youngsters into good baseball players – has in its way met with a lively interest on the part of the youngsters.

It is not difficult then to identify common views

cutting like highways through all the different social classes, just as here at home it is not difficult to identify the lack of divided opinions on modernist poetry or certain aspects of tax law. But what is important is that these shared views do not in any way contribute to the erosion of the bitter frontiers between the rival groups within the population. The hatred between the farmers and the city people has already been mentioned, and the even greater hatred between the poor city people evacuated to the country, whose distress is every bit as acute as that of the people left in the cities, and the farmers, who this autumn were still bartering food for clothes and linen but when inflation in the value of clothes and linen set in, even in the countryside, then wanted gold, silver and watches in return for potatoes, eggs and butter. The class divisions between the poor and the least poor have also been mentioned, the rising irritation between refugees and residents, and the reckless rivalry between competing political parties.

But there is another antagonism which is perhaps more fateful than any other: antagonism between the generations, the mutual contempt between youth and middle-age, excluding youth from the trade union leadership, from party leadership, and from executive ranks of the democratic institutions.

The absence of young people from political, labour and cultural life cannot be attributed simply to the inability of Nazified youth to interest itself in democratic undertakings. Within the parties and the unions young people are fighting their elders in a vain struggle for influence, which the older generations will not hand over to the younger, who, they say, have grown up in the shadow of the swastika, and which the younger in their turn will not entrust to the older, who, they say, bear the responsibility for the collapse of the old democracy. The defeat of the young results in a disillusioned and fateful predisposition against all forms of democratic organization, which are increasingly seen as something for old people.

What is remarkable about this generation conflict, however, is the fact that the representatives of the older generation are so old and those of the younger generation are in many cases no longer young. In the trade unions you can watch the fruitless struggles of a thirty-five-year-old against the sixty-year-olds; men who were radical youths before 1933 and did not shift their opinions during the Nazi years find it as hard to get a hearing as the youngsters who have known nothing other than Nazism. It is not altogether unjustified, in certain parts of Germany, to talk about a crisis in the parties and in the unions, and one of the main causes of this crisis is the fact that survivors of the 1933 collapse were too quick to grasp the rudder with their shaking old-man's hands.

The most tragic aspect of the big meeting under canvas which I attended in Frankfurt-am-Main just before Christmas and where the old Social Democrat and former Parliamentary President Paul Löbe spoke, was not perhaps that it was impossible to spot a single young person in the thousand-strong audience. What was tragic and frightening was that the audience were so advanced in years. About eighty per cent of those present were old men with woeful faces and frozen smiles who had come here to reminisce, not to find inspiration for the struggle to bring a new democracy to birth. The eighty per cent stood there round the arena while music bellowed from a loudspeaker and they mumbled The Internationale, and in the chilly silence round their dried-up voices, dry after thirteen years of silence, I had the unpleasant sensation of finding myself in a museum for a lost revolution and an equally lost generation. And outside the big tent youngsters had stood pointing the way with a sarcastic phrase: '*Hier geht alles nach rechts!*' Here everyone goes to the right!

German youth are in a tragic situation. They attend schools where slates have been nailed over the windows, schools where there is nothing to write on and nothing to read. These are the most ignorant children in the world, declared the young medical officer in Essen. From their school-yards they have a view over an endless panorama of ruins, and in the worst cases the ruins have to serve as school lavatories. Every day the teachers preach about the immorality of the black market, but when those youngsters go home they are forced by their own hunger and by their parents' hunger to take to the streets to find something to eat. This creates a terrible conflict, whose insolubility does nothing towards bridging the gap between the generations. It would be absurdly optimistic to imagine one could find such youngsters in any of the organizations of the dawning democracy. One has to face the naked reality and admit that German youth have their own organizations: the robber-gangs and the black-market centres.

Lost Generation

Germany has not just one lost generation, but many. One can argue about which is the most lost but never about which is the most regrettable. Those aged around twenty hang about the railway stations of small German towns long into the gathering darkness without having a train, or anything else, to wait for. Here one can observe small, desperate attempts at robbery carried out by nervous striplings who toss their heads defiantly when caught, or drunk school-girls clinging to Allied soldiers or half lying on waiting-room benches with drunk Negroes. No young generation has experienced such a fate, declares a well-known German publisher in a book written for and about this generation: they had conquered the world at eighteen and now at twenty-two they have lost everything.

In Stuttgart, where it is difficult to identify the remains of a lost beauty behind blackened façades, a meeting is held one evening for this the most regrettable of all lost generations. The meeting is held in a little church hall with space for about a hundred and fifty people and for the first and last time during my stay in Germany I saw a gathering with a full house, with participants who were not indifferent to what was happening, with a public that included young people: pale and destitute with hungry faces and ragged clothes, intellectual youngsters with fervent voices, young girls with a frightening hardness in their features, a rich arrogant young fellow in a fur collar who begins to smell American when he lights a cigarette. The chairman of the city's 'Young Democrats', who have arranged the meeting, introduces and welcomes a small, pale old man: this is one of the city's denazification lawyers.

'Many young people today are drifting in uncertainty,' says the chairman. 'Young people who belonged to the Hitler Youth or were forced into the SS and now today have to go without work on account of their past will this evening have a chance to question a representative of *die Spruchkammern* [the denazification courts] about the principles on which punishment is dealt out to members of their age-group.'

The old lawyer seems at first to be a typical example of those German lawyers who carry out their denazification duties with demonstrative reluctance. He emphasizes his reluctance by calling attention to the fact that the relevant law is American.

'We are lawyers,' he says. 'Don't spit on us. We must obey because the capitulation of Germany was unconditional and the Allies can do what they like with us. It's no good trying to sabotage *die Spruchkammern*. It's no good trying to falsify *die Fragebogen* [a kind of ideological equivalent of tax returns]. That only makes it worse for us and for you, since the Americans know who have been Nazis and who have not been. You complain that we work slowly, but in

Stuttgart alone the courts must deal with 120,000 people. You write letters complaining that you are going to be sentenced even if you don't admit yourselves guilty of any action to the benefit of Nazism. I answer – you promised the Führer unconditional loyalty and obedience. Wasn't that an action? You swore blind obedience to a man you didn't know. You paid four hundred marks a year in party subscriptions. Wasn't that an action?'

The lawyer is suddenly interrupted by an excited youngster:· 'But Hitler was a man the whole world recognized. Statesmen came here and signed treaties. The Pope was the first to recognize him. I've seen a picture showing the Pope shaking hands with him.'

The lawyer: 'I can't summon the Pope to my *Spruchkammer*.'

A young student: 'No one helped us, not the professors, who now have so much to say. Not you lawyers, who are now going to condemn us. I'm a lawyer too. As a lawyer I accuse the older generation of supporting Nazism through silence.'

A young soldier: 'All soldiers had to swear obedience to the Führer.'

The lawyer: 'But Party members did it voluntarily.'

The soldier: 'The responsibility is not ours, it doesn't lie with the young people.'

The lawyer: 'Never before in Germany has there been a party which demanded of its members that they should sign an undertaking of unqualified obedience.'

Excited voices: 'No? Herr Staatsanwalt, look at today's democratic parties!' (These youngsters are in fact quite honestly convinced that membership of a party unconditionally entails the duty of obedience towards a leader.)

The lawyer: 'It was an outrage, something unpardonable, a punishable offence, which today can be rewarded with six months' imprisonment, and for officials up to five years.'

Excited voices: 'No one told us that. We were fourteen then, Herr Advocat.'

The lawyer: 'I have spoken with people who have more experience than you have and they were appalled that this could happen. Each person who has signed the undertaking of obedience has put himself in a perilous situation. You can be grateful that the Allies have come here. Would it be better if there had been a revolution and you had lost your heads?'

The rich young fellow: 'Then we wouldn't need any vitamins, Herr Staatsanwalt!'

The lawyer: 'The law is a piece of good luck for you as former National Socialists. The law is mild since it takes account of youth, and youth, I may add, does not involve freedom from responsibility. You are responsible in the same way for a flower-pot that tumbles down from your window-ledge.'

The student: 'Herr Advocat, let me say that you, the older generation, who kept silent are responsible for our fate in the same way as a mother who lets her children starve to death.'

The lawyer: 'You know that those of you who were born after 1919 can be given an amnesty – that is, if you don't belong to the most tainted category – those who made themselves guilty of maltreatment and violence. Besides, we who are older must also admit that Nazism did not deal improperly with youth. There are young people who look back with joy to their Hitler Youth days.' (Murmurs of agreement.)

'And one must remember as well that there was a dictatorship not only in Germany, but also in Turkey, in Spain and in Italy.'

'Don't forget Russia, Herr Advocat,' someone calls out, then quotes word for word from a Churchill speech about Russian politics, 'In that respect even the Nazis fell short.'

The lawyer: 'The law applies to the entire population. It's not a matter simply of paying a fine of a couple of thousand marks and being done with it. A mental readjustment is demanded, on the part of the younger generation as well. Don't say any longer "We can't do anything", no matter how true it may be that no group of young people have been treated worse than you have been.'

Middle-aged SS man: 'The first sensible word this evening!'

The lawyer: 'The young and the old are in the same boat. Do we have a chance of bettering our lot?'

The audience: 'Yes, we have – through us.'

The lawyer: 'Do you think that the politicians in Paris can help us, running from one conference to the next without anything being achieved? It's we who have to help ourselves. We must have patience. It was not only Germany that had unemployment in 1933, but it was Germany that had no time to wait. Now we must learn patience, for reconstruction needs patience.'

The Chairman: 'Herr Advocat, weren't we young people in the Hitler years inspired with a will to construct?'

The SS man: 'We were idealists, Herr Staatsanwalt. We demand an amnesty for SS men. Everyone here knows how a young fellow became an SS man.

Someone said "Karl, you're a fine tall chap, you're for the SS" – and so Karl was in the SS. Everyone fights for his country and regards that as something creditable, so why should we be punished for having fought for our Germany?'

The lawyer: 'We lawyers are bound to our professional duty. The denazification law is our employer. Even I myself am slowly coming, it seems, to be regarded as nazified. The Americans have taken my house, my furniture too. So blame the law, not *die Spruchkammern*. Remember that we older people did not have a much easier time than you did. For twelve years we stood with one foot in the concentration camp and for the last six years the threat of bombing was over our heads both day and night. Not just youth but the whole German people are sick: sick of inflation, reparations, unemployment and Hitlerism. That's too much for a people aged twenty-five. We lawyers have no prescription for recovery. We can do only one thing: try to apply the most lenient interpretations of the law, try to move the most tainted into the group of the less tainted; and be certain that we are doing all we can. We are doing our utmost for the younger generation, but in the first instance we are lawyers and according to the terms of the capitulation we cannot refuse to take due notice of the laws governing denazification.'

And with this apologetic flourish the old lawyer concluded. He should have held an introductory address which without any discussion ought to have brought him thus far, but he was not able to hold out against the vehement opposition which kept invading his carefully composed speech and breaking it apart.

70

It was fascinating to observe how this practised and well-bred man simply did not dare to use the customary style of parliamentary retort against this excited opposition. In fact we often meet in the older generation a physical dread of youth and this is one of the reasons why the older ranks of political and public life deal so restrictively with youth and at a safe distance.

In the following discussion the young audience listened without interest as the SS men spoke about the bloody First of May in 1929 and about the bloody internecine strife among the parties of the left. The student-lawyer had a special problem. His 'taint' lay ten years back in time. He had become a Pg (*Partei genosse*, Party member) in 1936 at the age of twenty-three and then in maturer years had 'denazified himself', but now he was being summoned to appear. The lawyer replied that of course it would be desirable if all young people were to receive individual treatment but that nothing could now be done about that.

The student: 'We young lawyers were forced to join the Party. Who would have helped us if we had refused? Many young lawyers in Hessen have now been put on the street with their families and left to whistle for work. Without the younger generation there is no democracy, but if we are treated like this then we just lose all interest in doing anything at all for democracy.'

At this stage the rich young fellow brightens up and calls out 'Bravo!' The lawyer consoles his young colleague by pointing out that only the accused of Class One, that is, war criminals, can be punished

71

with exclusion from work, but a young woman protests and claims that employers who have perhaps themselves been Pg turn up their noses when they hear that an applicant for a job is a young Pg. These employers are afraid of the newly introduced management councils, representing the new industrial democracy, which she maintains are much worse than *die Spruchkammern*.

And she is no doubt right. The whole of Germany either laughs at or weeps over this business of denazification, this comedy where *die Spruchkammern* play a lamentable double role as the friend in need, those courts whose lawyers apologize to the accused before judgement falls, these enormous paper-mills where it can happen that an accused person in this Germany of paper shortages turns up with a hundred testimonials proving his unimpeachability and wades through thousands of meaningless and trivial instances while the really important instances somehow vanish through a secret trap-door.

This young generation melting away into the Stuttgart night faces a worse fate than any previous one, and in the little drama in which it took part this evening it has perhaps not told the truth about itself or the truth about the events in which willingly or unwillingly it participated, but one thing is clear: it has told the truth about what it thinks of itself and what it thinks of a generation by whom it is both feared and despised in this sad prelude to winter, when big red placards on the walls of ruins promise a reward of fifty thousand marks for information leading to the arrest of those responsible for the attack on Stuttgart's *Spruchkammer*.

The Course of Justice

There is a lack of happiness in post-war Germany but
no lack of entertainments. Every day the cinemas run
their films to packed houses, all day until nightfall,
and they have introduced standing-room in order to
meet the demand. On their programmes we can find
Allied war films, while in the meantime American
experts in militarism search with magnifying glasses
for militaristic tendencies in German literature. The
theatres probably have the best repertoire in northern
Europe and the most eager public in the world, and
the dance halls, where for the sake of hygiene the
Allied military police make a couple of raids per
evening, find their square metres of floor-space
overpopulated. But amusing oneself is expensive.
Theatre tickets cost cheap time and dear money. Free
amusements are rare and must be taken where they
are to be found.

A fairly common amusement, in its way, in the
American zone, is to attend a *Spruchkammersitzung*,
that is, a session of a denazification court. The man
with the rustling sandwich-paper, who with unfailing
interest watches case after case rolling past before his
seldom wearying eyes, is one of the regulars in the

naked courts in half-bombed palaces of justice which lack even a relic of the sadistic elegance with which justice otherwise loves to surround itself. It would be wrong to think that the man with the sandwiches is drawn to the court to savour the tardy triumph of definitive justice. He is more likely to be a theatre enthusiast who has come here to satisfy his craving for the stage. At its best, that is when the prosecutors and the defenders are sufficiently interesting, a *Spruch-kammersitzung* is really a stately and engrossing piece of drama: with its rapid shifts from past to present, its endless questioning of witnesses where not one tiny action on the part of the accused in the course of the relevant twelve years is considered too trivial to be passed over, the performance can seem like an example of applied existentialism. The atmosphere of dream and unreality in which this ransacking of a whole nation's regrettable or terrifying memories is carried out has literary associations too. We could well have been transported to the scenes of Kafka's *The Trial*: these court-rooms with their half bricked-up windows, their bomb-damaged furniture, and their position high up under the holed roof, are like an illustration from reality of the desolate attic offices where *The Trial* unwinds.

It is characteristic of the entire situation that a matter so fundamentally serious as denazification should immediately become an event for a theatre critic. But for a stranger, of course, these brief trials, as a rule concluded in a few hours, generate a special interest because with a rare sharpness they give a picture of conditions in the Hitler years, of the motives of those who became Nazis and the courage of those who did not. From the questioning of the witnesses we can feel a cold draught from the time of terror, a fragment of history so far invisible can flare into life for a few short, charged moments and make the air tremble in the raw court-room. For anyone not personally caught up in those desperate years these trials have a terrible documentary fascination, but as a means of denazification they are quite useless. On that point we must accept an opinion universally held by the Germans themselves.

There is indeed a touching unanimity as to the ridiculous and infuriating forms taken by this process. The former Nazis talk provokingly about a barbaric collective punishment. Others think that fines of a few hundred marks are hardly the depth of barbarity but maintain that it is a pure waste of labour keeping this giant apparatus functioning for the sake of minor Party members when the big ones run free. The conveyor-belt technique also undoubtedly gives a dangerous air of the ridiculous to the whole principle of denazification. It was typical of the resulting attitude that in their election propaganda the Communists, parodying the title of Fallada's well-known novel – *Kleiner Mann – was nun?* became *Kleiner Pg – was nun?* – should turn to the small fry of the Nazi Party whose dislike of denazification they tried to collect. According to current usage, moreover, *Spruchkammer* is no longer called *Spruchkammer*, but either *Bruchkammer* (*Bruch* meaning 'kaputt') or *Sprichkammer* (*Sprich* meaning 'talk').

But talk can also be of interest to anyone wanting to know the truth about the history of those twelve years. One day begins with a humble schoolteacher and ends with a corrupt Nazi official. This is in

Frankfurt-am-Main, where *die Spruchkammer* for once is better than its reputation. This is because there are judges here who are not ashamed of their job, who do not bow and scrape to the accused and who do not mince their words.

The schoolteacher has been summoned as a 'less tainted' case. He belonged to the SA but in general did not shine there. He is a well-mannered pale little man who answers all the questions like a Sunday school pupil. He tells the court about his childhood, which was poor and dismal, and about his lifelong desire to be a schoolteacher. He was well on the way to becoming one when Nazism arrived and he was then faced with the bitter choice: dutifully join some Nazi organization and realize his ambition, or give up his future.

'It was only after great doubts and after long deliberations with my father that I decided to enter such an organization.'

'But why exactly the SA?'

'Because it seemed to me that the SA were the least blameworthy.'

'*Die Strasse frei den braunen Bataillonen* – do you call that blameless?' the judge wonders.

But the accused has six witnesses to declare that he is innocent, witnesses who swear that they have never heard him reveal a Nazi turn of mind, witnesses who certify that he listened to foreign radio stations (all of the accused have done that), Jewish witnesses who have seen him behaving in a friendly manner towards Jews (all of the accused have such witnesses – they cost a couple of hundred marks apiece), and a headmaster who certainly never attended any of his lessons but yet is remarkably well-informed about

76

them, and at last a girl from the training college library who declares that the accused is truth-loving, self-sacrificing, dutiful, careful with books and kind towards children and dogs, and who has a small fit of tears when the judge tells her brusquely that that is irrelevant. What weighed most in the acquittal of the schoolteacher was the fact that he conducted a church choir for a whole year after any kind of church activity could be compromising. Even the prosecutor intervenes on behalf of the accused and the case is over.

Then come two typical routine cases, deserving only a sort of absent-minded disappointed response on the part of the man with the sandwich-packet, cases as commonplace as the names of the accused: Müller and Krause. Herr Müller has been a workplace representative for the unsuccessful Nazi trade union movement which over several years and with surprising lack of progress the Nazis tried to stir into life, but witnesses testify that at least he was not guilty of agitation with threats. But on two occasions he wore the union uniform, one of which was on the Saviour's birthday. On the other hand he has of course listened to foreign radio stations and been kind to a Jewish family. He is sentenced to make reparations to the tune of two thousand marks. The uniform is declared forfeit, and the accused is further fined one suit and one pair of shoes.

Herr Krause has listened to foreign radio stations and had a Jewish cousin. Herr Krause, who joined the Party in 1940, is a small, coughing accountant with nervous glasses that ceaselessly wander between his nose and the table. Herr Krause has sixteen long testimonials from the bank management, from bank colleagues, from neighbours, from a doctor who treated him, from a lawyer who had handled his divorce. Herr Krause reads them all out in a soporific nasal voice while the court slowly drifts to sleep and all that can be heard is the rustling of sandwich-paper at the back of the big room.

Why did Herr Krause become a Nazi in 1940?

The testimonials say that it was a matter of divorce proceedings which had begun in 1930 and, unchecked by the onset of Nazism, had dragged on, so that by 1939 Herr Krause was poor and ulcerous. By 1940, driven to the point of despair and passed over to the advantage of colleagues who were Party men, Herr Krause decided to take the repugnant step.

The judge intervened here:

'It didn't perhaps have something to do with the fact that in 1940 France was defeated, Herr Krause, and you found it convenient to show your sympathy for the victor, since this would in all likelihood guarantee you a position with a considerably higher salary?'

No, of course not. Herr Krause is no *Nutzniesser* (profiteer), Herr Krause would not take advantage of any apparent victory. Yes – apparent. One did listen to foreign broadcasts. Moreover while Herr Krause was certainly promoted he had to perform his duties in a bank on the eastern front, 'and, My Lord, for a man with my weak stomach . . .' No, Herr Krause was simply ill and poor, and something had to be done to avoid a catastrophe. One simply has to look at the testimonials.

In the meantime the defence lawyer is leafing through a thick decree. With a triumphant smile he at last begs permission to speak. It has perhaps not been made clear in the testimonials, but Herr Krause is in fact still employed by the same bank, which is now working for the occupying powers, and according to the denazification law Germans employed by the military government cannot be accused of Nazism.

'For is it likely, My Lord, that the Americans would appoint a suspected person, and in, may I add, such an important post?'

The court falls silent and in the deathly stillness a thick and invisible blanket of censorship settles softly over the proceedings. The case against Herr Krause is promptly dropped. Herr Krause – small, nervous, humble, ever-dutiful, with his divorce and his bad stomach, wedging his glasses on his nose, gathering together his sixteen typewritten testimonials and stuffing them into his shining briefcase, a kindly, hunched little man who bows to the judge, the assessors, the defence lawyer and the prosecutor – then hurries off out of the court-room, just as fearful of arriving late for his bank duties in 1947 as he was in 1924, in 1933, in 1940 and near Stalingrad in 1942.

Then comes Herr Sinne and he is not a kindly man. Herr Sinne is seventy-three years old: fragile, white-haired and with his doll-like head looking like a pensioner-angel. But Herr Sinne is no angel. Herr Sinne is summoned as an activist. He was a section leader in Frankfurt, and no testimonials to the effect that he was nice to Jews or listened to English broadcasts can help him. The court has testimony that Herr Sinne has said: 'My section will be free of Jews.' The court has witnesses who can tell that Herr Sinne threatened to report shopkeepers in his section if they dared to sell groceries to Jewish customers. It was only after closing time that the Jewish witnesses could sneak into the shops from the back and buy what they needed. A woman witness has often seen Herr Sinne listening at the letter-box of a Jewish girl-friend of hers. The son of a Herr Meyer, whose balcony could be observed from Herr Sinne's window, had one evening stood on the balcony with a Jewish girl. Next day Herr Meyer had a reminder from Herr Sinne that he should not have Jews on his balcony.

Meanwhile Herr Sinne is sitting there letting his squirrel-eyes dart between the witnesses, and perhaps it is just an optical illusion but there is a sudden impression that Herr Sinne is surrounded by a membrane of cold dread, this dried-up old-man's body radiates a deathly chill that sends shivers through a spectator ten metres away.

One of the Jewish witnesses relates:

'A high Party official lived in Herr Sinne's section but we were never afraid of him. We were always afraid of Herr Sinne. Herr Sinne was not one of the Nazi highlights, but Herr Sinne was one of those quiet, dependable, terribly effective cogs without which the Nazi machine would not have kept going for one day.'

Herr Sinne gets up slowly.

'Herr Cohn, you always greeted me in such a friendly way every day,' he says shrilly. 'You never looked as if you had anything to complain of.'

'Herr Sinne,' says the judge mildly, 'I am convinced that many people greeted you courteously because they were frightened of you.'

'Frightened of me? A sick old man!'

'Just look at this ageing face,' cries out the defence lawyer pathetically. 'Does it look as if it could frighten anyone?'

One of the women witnesses becomes hysterical.

'Think instead,' she screams, 'of the faces of the old Jewish men in Herr Sinne's section!'

Herr Sinne explains that everything is lies, the balcony in question is not visible from his window, he has never said that his section was to be free of Jews, and he has never forbidden anyone to shop in his section. The case is postponed for a week, and then the shopkeepers will be called in as witnesses, and Herr Sinne, all alone and with his gaze fixed on some point in the past goes his way with a childish seventy-three-year-old forehead raised proudly against the contempt murmuring behind him.

The Walter case is simple but interesting. Walter himself is a giant with a club-foot who the moment he enters throws his stick on the table and accuses the Hessen government of corruption, but he is bluntly silenced by the judge. Walter was an official in a Nazi commission and is accused of being an informer, but what is interesting is that Herr Walter is still in the same commission in 1946 and it is in 1946 that he has had enough money to buy a farm in Hessen. He has been reported by Herr Bauer, a fat and slow-witted horse-dealer who does not look as if he has gone hungry for one moment in the land of hunger. It soon turns out that the horse-dealer's motives are not as noble as they might have appeared. The two gentlemen have quite simply quarrelled with each other over an illegal consignment of oats, delivered to a nameless American major, of whose existence next day's newspaper report very properly remains silent. The horse-dealer then suddenly remembered his competitor's Nazism and reported him. The case is adjourned for lack of evidence, but the judge cannot forgo a sarcastic remark to the horse-dealer:

'The old masters were easier to deal with, weren't they?'

But the horse-dealer confidently replies: 'The new ones are all right too, My Lord.'

And what he says is true, and what is so hopeless and idiotic and tragic is that the new masters in commissions and in decision-making organs are in fact 'all right' for anyone who is sufficiently free of prejudice, for anyone who knows the art of wearing whatever colours he chooses. It is harder for the victims of Nazism because they meet obstacles everywhere. They have the right to seats in trains and priority in queues, but would never dare dream of making use of such a right, but for Messrs Walter and Bauer a providential power, often of American nationality, has placed redeeming trap-doors in the lamentable stage-boards of the denazification courts.

Cold Day in Munich

A Sunday in early winter in Munich, with a cold sun. The long Prinzregentenstrasse, from which one of the unhappiest heroes of world literature once started his journey towards death in Venice, lies deserted in the frosty morning light. There is nothing in the world so deserted and lonely as an empty main street on a cold morning in a bombed city. The sun glitters on the gold of the angel of peace, the angel of peace which divides Prinzregentenstrasse into two monumental gradual slopes down to the bridge over the Isar and which Hitler should have been able to view from his house on Prinzregentenplatz. The gardens in the old ambassadorial palaces lie full of tumbled pillars. On the newly frozen ice of the sports arena a few early-morning Americans are skating, but *die grüne Isar* is green as usual and far down under the bridge some bombs have made a jigsaw puzzle out of a pond.

The dirty Jeep lurches along the endless street. The severe-looking government building is there, between well-roasted façades of ruins; that is where

Minister-President Dr Högner spends several hours a day playing with the idea of letting Bavaria renounce its connection with the rest of Germany, according to a theory which says that Prussia has twice brought Bavaria to a state of ruin and should not be allowed the chance of doing so a third time. Bavaria, cold-bloodedly sending evacuees from Hamburg, Hannover and Essen back to the total impossibilities of their native cities, is of course a selfish, hard-hearted and tough region, but that is not the whole truth. At least a quarter of the truth is that Bavaria has no feeling of belonging to the rest of Germany and that – in spite of a general belief to the contrary – there was a not insignificant degree of passive resistance to Nazism in Bavaria.

But not far from Prinzregentenstrasse lie the ruins of the Brown House. The first bloody Hitler putsch was played out in Munich in 1923 and the remains of Bürgerbräukeller still testify that the history of Nazism has deep roots here. No doubt, says the humorous native of Munich, but perhaps that is because of the föhn in spring, that wind from the mountains which gives the whole of Munich an intolerable month-long headache; he points out too that after the Nazis had made it compulsory for pedestrians to bare their heads as they passed Feldherrenhalle, where the memorial to the sixteen victims of the putsch was set up, the density of the pedestrian traffic in that once so thronging part of Munich noticeably diminished.

On Prinzregentenstrasse lies too *die Export-Schau*, accommodated in one of those sexless pseudo-classical Hitler buildings which do not look ancient until they are ruins. The Export Exhibition is a sadistic arrangement where the city authorities, with a remarkable psychological insight and for an entry fee of one mark, display what Bavarian industry can achieve, that is, what Bavarian industry can export to America. There, bombed-out housewives can look at fine dream-like porcelain they will never eat off; big bottles stand full of real German beer which one can no longer drink; and lengths of splendid fabrics hang which one is forbidden to touch. For anyone poor and hungry this must feel like landing up in a disastrous dream, where everything is certainly unreal as in a dream, but where the dreamer is constantly aware of his own hunger and his own poverty.

II

A few minutes away from Prinzregentenstrasse is Königsplatz, that desert built by the architects of Nazism, which more than most other examples of the type reveals the lack of style, the desolation and the patent sadism of the Nazi ideals. One enters through narrow openings in a broken triumphal arch or between the two elevated marble tombs of the sixteen Munich martyrs, where their zinc coffins, eight in each grave, lay buried until the Americans on their arrival moved them to an unknown alternative site. The former graves are flanked by two huge palaces, characteristic buildings of the Hitler period, that look like mausoleums in honour not of any particular death but of death itself as a principle. In one of these mausoleums the Munich Agreement of 1933 was signed. At that time the triumphal arch was still whole and it is easy to close one's eyes and imagine how the cavalcade of the signatories' cars came through the

85

arch and in a gentle curve over the square approached the monumental tomb-like buildings, where for the moment the world's destiny lay buried, and today on this cold morning in early winter something is going to happen which for an hour or two will conjure the dead from their graves.

Below the triumphal arch a brass band is assembling. The cold sunlight glitters from the instruments, the breath from the mouths of the players is white. You walk across this endless square, whose surface of huge ashlar stones gives a curious impression of being indoors, into the vast entry-hall of the locked castle like those we have dreams about. The heavy American lorries sweeping along the white traffic-ways in under the arch appear quite unreal in these surroundings. A few hundred stamping and shivering people have gathered before the band; there is an American woman correspondent in uniform, one of those strange creatures who seem to have been born wearing a camera; two lorries have driven round behind the band in such a way that standing there back to back they form a platform for journalists and speakers. A steady stream of people is flowing in, and by ten o'clock ten thousand stand waiting.

The band plays a march, sounding rough in the cold. The journalists of Munich sharpen their pencils, representatives of those remarkable and courageous papers that largely without telephones or typewriters or offices still manage in some mysterious way to appear, printed in cellars ankle-deep with water on rainy days (the printers having to wade about in wellingtons) – those same newspapers that, comically, at the wish of the Americans are 'above party', which has meant that more than one confused Herr

Müller has read in the Monday edition of his local chronicle a Social Democrat leader prescribing the greatest suspicion towards the Christian Socialists, and then on Wednesday in the same chronicle a Christian Socialist leader exhorting readers to watch out for the Social Democrats, and then on Friday, still in the same chronicle, a Communist leader issuing an urgent warning against both the Social Democrats and the Christian Socialists.

So, the journalists are sharpening their pencils, in the loudspeakers one man welcomes another man, the voices die away and the music falls silent. A man who has taken off his overcoat rises and walks stiffly over the platform. The silence intensifies even further, something of the tension before a revolver shot about to be fired trembles in the cold air above Königsplatz. The man behind the microphone is Dr Kurt Schumacher, leader of the German Social Democrats.

Then when he starts speaking the spell breaks. We can see why he took off his overcoat. Dr Schumacher is a speaker who can talk in his jacket in a temperature of minus ten without feeling cold. At the Kästner Cabaret in Schau-Bude there is a Schumacher caricature: a new Führer who waves his arms and howls with the same hysteria as the old one. The caricature is inaccurate to the extent that its new Führer has two arms. Dr Schumacher has only one but his manner of using it is fascinating. And it is not quite true that Dr Schumacher screams. The impression he makes is due rather to his restrained passion, his sulkiness, the absolute lack of sentimentality in his tone, which allows him to utter sentimentalities that sound like bitter truths, and his sour crossness, which can so easily be taken for reliability and which sometimes allows him to tell half-truths that sound like whole-truths.

Dr Schumacher is regarded even by his opponents as a respectable personality and without doubt he has a kind of honest boldness, yet in his way he embodies the thesis that the German politician's tragedy is that he is such a good speaker. One gets the impression that Dr Schumacher is seduced by his public, that the bold phrases pouring out of him are a result of an interplay between his own and the public's feelings rather than of his own carefully considered political experience.

Of course he cannot have avoided noticing that his position is exposed, perilous even, to the extent that he becomes a medium for feelings that are fundamentally not in accordance with the political lines of his party. It would be naïve to suppose that they are Social Democrats, those ten thousand in Königsplatz who rejoice when Dr Schumacher apostrophizes 'the seven million absent comrades' (the POWs), when he dwells on the shameful Munich Agreement (a most effective thing to dwell on when one has ten thousand listeners with their backs to the very building where it was signed), when he demands the return of the Saar, the return of the Ruhr, East Prussia and Silesia. It is also an illusion, and a more regrettable one, to think that the majority of those ten thousand care one jot for the democratic ideals which Dr Schumacher purposes, among other things, to represent.

The explanation of Dr Schumacher's successes as a politician and the explanation of why together with Churchill he has taken the place in many doubtful German hearts obviously left vacant at the collapse, is that he has managed to find a common wavelength on which more or less all Germans, independently of their political leanings, can be gathered. The one-sidedness in Dr Schumacher's political preaching makes it acceptable also to Germans who have not yet overcome their Nazism and do not really want to overcome it either. If we accept the reasonable supposition that Dr Schumacher's case is one where a public seduces a much too clever talker then the phenomenon shows itself here in Munich in the way in which, right from the start, the speaker fends off any kind of objection on the part of his public, that is, stubbornly concentrates on those territorial injustices which even the most indifferent German mass must find disturbing. Only once does a small protest roll up from the sea of heads. It comes from a Communist who wants to let the Russians keep East Prussia.

'It's me they've come to listen to, not you,' replies Dr Schumacher with cross humour and gets nine thousand seven hundred laughers on his side.

Dr Schumacher is without doubt good for his party, but the question is whether he is too good, that is, dangerous – dangerous not primarily because of his views, which are not just his own but are expressed with equal openness by Neumann in Berlin, by Paul Löbe and by other Social Democrat leaders, but most dangerous because of his enormous popularity, which will perhaps win election victories for his party – but what kind of victories?

It can be seen as a pious and risky piece of self-deception when German Social Democracy presents its electoral progress as proof that democratic attitudes are on the increase in the German people.

Among those who vote for the Social Democrats there are still a considerable number who are without doubt captivated by the idea of asserting German nationalist views by way of voting for a democratic party and such a supposition is confirmed by the important difference between the voting figures for the parties and their real strength. It is worth remembering that in an average German city while the ratio of Social Democrat figures to those of the Communists is six to one, that between their respective memberships is more like three to two.

When his speech is finished one notices how helpless this tall, fragile man with the sad face really is. The speech has supported, the speech has warmed him, now suddenly he sinks, and someone comes and wraps a scarf round his neck and helps him on with his overcoat. Alone, he makes his way through the crowd towards his car. People call greetings to him which he ignores. People storm him with questions which he does not answer. He is due to travel to England next day and someone shouts 'Don't forget to say that in London too, Dr Schumacher!' Dr Schumacher nods but does not smile. Dr Schumacher generally does not smile – Dr Schumacher who has won the confidence of a whole people through smiling as little as possible, Dr Schumacher who has given so many Germans the chance of voting democratically without their needing to be democrats, while indeed being quite the opposite. Dr Schumacher has of course not chosen this, but his frontier propaganda, in many ways reasonable but ideologically much too superficial, has had this result.

This most gifted of contemporary German politicians, who at the same time is the one with the cleanest hands, can hardly be accused on account of his views on the injustices committed against Germany by the Allied politicians: paralysing production through badly organized dismantling schemes; giving Germans charity in the form of provisions instead of helping peacetime production to its feet and thus giving Germans the chance of paying for their imports; using POWs for forced labour, which breaks the Hague Convention and is a highly unsuitable way of teaching the German people to respect it in the future; imposing the strikingly rigid frontier regulations that threaten vital German interests. If a German socialist who suffered more or perhaps longer under Nazi-German oppression than the socialists of any other country should express such thoughts, that is no more unjustifiable than is the case when for example an English liberal like Gollancz offers to interpret them.

What can be held against Dr Schumacher is that through his doomsday sermons against the victors he adopts a limited national perspective instead of a socialist and internationalist one. It can be objected that there are justified national claims which have nothing to do with nationalism or chauvinism. But hasn't the German fate demonstrated how the dividing-line between propaganda for national interests and the rancorously manifested nationalism of Nazi Germany is one that seems to exist in order to be crossed? Should it not be a part of a democratic training to teach the otherwise rare art of keeping that line uncrossed? It can also be held against Dr Schumacher that he cultivates a type of propaganda which is only too easily received by German nationalists. Give them a dose of socialism, democracy and internationalism – and Dr Schumacher will be less popular but more fitted to speak for the new-born democracy.

Through the Forest of
the Hanged Boys

The forests heal their wounds more quickly than anything else. Here and there, of course, among the oaks there is an unemployed field-gun whose broken barrel stares morosely at the ground as if ashamed. The shells of small brown cars lie on the slopes like huge food-cans. Untidy camper-giants have been moving in a hurry through these the most assiduously well-managed of the world's forests. Still, the war has made its way most considerately between the trees and through the little villages: the latter experienced the bombing of the cities only as a kind of red aurora at night and felt the ground tremble and doors and windows rattle. The occasional house was, naturally, knocked out by mistake, and at this point the local tragedy would be concentrated. In the small village by the Weser it was a dentist's house that was hit one spring morning during surgery hours and the dentist, the nurse and all thirty patients were killed. Out in the garden a man was walking to and fro waiting while his daughter had a tooth pulled inside the house, and in the waiting-room sat his wife and his mother, who had also accompanied the girl to the dentist's so that she would not feel afraid. The man escaped as by a

93

miracle but his whole family was lost, and for the past couple of years he has been going round the village like a wandering Second World War memorial – the First World War memorial is to be found in a little grove between the bank of the Weser and the first house and is still the pride of the village.

Like the forests, the villages have had time to lick their wounds. The wreckage of the dentist's villa has been cleared up but when the Sunday cinema is over people often saunter past the site and reminisce on the event, or they go up to the abutment of the bridge and stand gazing down at the autumn waters swirling round the pier-stumps. The bridge was blown up by hysterical SS lads at about five minutes past twelve. Their hated memory is still intensely alive in the village. '*Oh – sie haben gew-ü-ü-ü-tet*' – Oh, they were furious, almost worse than the Poles.

The defeat trailed through the main street of the village for two whole days: ragged and muddy soldiers from the Wehrmacht on bicycles or on foot and last in the queue the young boys and old men of the Great Assault, sniffling and stumbling through the mire of defeat. Of the victors people remember especially the dashing Scotsmen, about a dozen of whom lie buried in a piece of ground sloping towards the river, under white crosses bright as spring flowers in the wet autumn gloom. The village children play war-games in the porches of the cold overpopulated houses along with tattered refugee children from the eastern zone or from Sudetenland. Children in villages get up late in the mornings, trying to cheat the stomach into sleeping past a meal they cannot have. If one shows them a picture-book they will unfailingly begin to consult each other as to how they can best beat to death the human figures or the animals shown on the pages. Small boys who have been twice bombed out of home, who can scarcely yet speak properly, pronounce the word '*totschlagen*' with gruesome precision.

In the course of a single year the village by the Weser has had its population increased tenfold and new inhabitants are arriving all the time at these little brick houses which are already inflamed by the hate, envy and hunger of the overcrowded. In a tiny hovel with greaseproof paper instead of glass in the window lives Henry, a Sudeten-German boy who lost part of a leg in the war on the Baltic but who this year lost his heart to the Englishmen he works for. He has been given a watch by his English major and he reads Edgar Wallace in English during the night when it is too cold to sleep. In another little ice-cold room a German-Hungarian girl is allowed to borrow a bed at night. Through the day she helps out at the village doctor's house or wanders around on the southern bank of the Weser longing for Budapest. She has twice tried to take her life with sleeping-pills. The whole household is now waiting for the third attempt.

Compared to the cities with their bleeding ruins, the German villages do look as if they have recovered, and the forests look in good shape, but this good health is only apparent. I spend a few days in a small village outside Darmstadt with an evacuated family in a tumbledown farm with neither land nor animals. This is reached through oak woodlands that cling to a gentle blue mountainside. A Roman cutting runs down the slope. The region is full of abandoned mills by romantically rustling streams. In a ditch there lies a blasted filing-cabinet from an old Wehrmacht store but there are no other wartime mementoes to be discovered. However, as we sit talking in the kitchen one evening there is a knock on the door and a little ruddy apple-cheeked boy comes in, wanting to play with the child who lives here, a small, thin five-year-old girl who has spent nearly every night for two years sitting in cellars. When asked if she would like a doll for Christmas instead of her old Seppelchen, which has endured as many cellar-nights as she has, she replies that she would rather have a sandwich with a really thick layer of butter. But that is only something to dream of. Now and then when she has been specially good she gets a sandwich with margarine and sugar, and even that kind of sandwich is something to dream of. But the boy who has come in does not need, it appears, to dream in vain of proper sandwiches.

'*Hänschen hat dicke Backen*,' says someone and Hänschen smiles confidently. Yes, little Hans really has chubby cheeks, and in his right hand little Hans is holding a big sandwich spread with goose-dripping. This turns out to be a pathetic confrontation between two kinds of sandwich, between two kinds of Germany: the poor but honest, the prosperous but dubious. Little Hans's father was prosecutor in a Nazi court but now he has retired from *die Blut* and gone over to *der Boden*. He has – please note, after the collapse of Germany – bought the biggest farm here and manages for himself a hundred times better than the evacuated ex-concentration-camp prisoners who were given quarters in the dilapidated and badly maintained cottages.

Are people bitter? Of course they are, but that helps no one. In the evenings we sit by the stove and talk about events past and present. Here is a Communist with nine years in Buchenwald for ever etched on his forehead and round his mouth and eyes. He laments the lost revolution, the great upheavel that would have blasted its cleansing fire over Germany and in a moment burnt up all the Nazi pollution which is now being allowed to thrive and make Germany still more dissatisfied, unhappy and worn-out. He maintains that the conditions existed, that in April 1945 the public mood was right for a short but intense reckoning. The soldiers who were pushed back over their own frontiers were embittered at the Hitler regime and would have done everything they could to get even. The crowds from the concentration camps were ready to cast themselves over their tormentors, and in the blitzed and battered cities there were strong anti-Nazi groups of activists who kept up a civil war with the Nazis throughout the spring of 1945. So why did nothing come of all this? The answer is – the victorious capitalistic nations of the West did not want an anti-Nazi revolution. The revolutionary groups in Germany were isolated from one another by the conquering armies instead of being allowed to form a defensive circle of guns round Germany's frontiers in order to let the Germans themselves settle their score with those they detested. The revolutionary masses from the concentration camps were sent home not all at once but in small harmless batches, the soldiers were released in very small contingents, and the resistance-groups in the cities, who were already busy with an often heavy-handed denazification before the war ended, were disarmed by the Allies and replaced

by the Boards of Appeal which allow Nazi prosecutors
to buy farms and anti-Nazi workers to starve to death.

This theory, which is entertained not only by
Communists, is very seductive and provides, among
other things, an interesting aspect of the Communist
thesis of a unity between the German Labour parties.
At the time of the actual collapse there were
undoubtedly possibilities for such a unity based
purely on anti-Nazi feelings but the longed-for
People's Front, also in its way a reality, soon came to
nothing. Its bourgeois components refused to co-
operate with the worker elements and divisions
appeared between the Social Democrats and the
Communists. The latter, who quite openly refuse no
chance of promoting themselves as a *German* party,
yet regard all POWs returning from the Soviet Union
as anti-Russian propaganda (though these can hardly
help looking undernourished), consider this outcome
as a German tragedy. But there are numerous
anti-Nazi Germans who had hoped for another
outcome: people who reject the kind of unity without
freedom offered by the Communists regret that the
anti-Nazi enthusiasm of the spring of 1945 failed to
create something other than the ensuing situation of
party division and impotence in the face of reaction.
The twelve-year-old dream of a revolution died and
the Weimar men were born again.

People are therefore bitter, disillusioned and hopeless. They are bitter because of the two unequal
sandwiches and because of many other small things of
vital importance. We stand outside the house for a
time in the twilight and look up at the hawk-like
profile of Berg Frankenstein in the mist. We stand

and look at the forest, which I have come through only yesterday, and one of us says that not even the forest is as innocent as it seems. There in April 1945 defiant boys who were running home to mum from the Great Assault were hanged. Little Hans '*mit den dicken Backen*' has eaten up his sandwich and is playing among the oaks with the thin little five-year-old. The prosecutor-turned-farmer is driving home the day's last load of firewood from his forest. This year he waves a friendly greeting to those whom two years ago, he had helped to condemn. He even salutes with his whip. An American irony! – a Nazi lawyer fetches his firewood out of the forest where scarcely two years ago the Nazis hanged children. And high above the oaks, nearly up on Berg Frankenstein, comes the sharp hard noise of rifle-fire in the dusk. It is the Americans up there, lying on the mountain above the forest of the hanged boys and shooting wild pig with the victor's ammunition.

Return to Hamburg

'America.'

'*Bitte?*'

'America!'

'America?'

'*Jawohl.*'

There's no doubting him. The boy wants to go to America and nothing can be done about it. Nothing but shake one's head and stare helplessly up into the broken roof's cloudy ironwork in the darkness high above us. But the boy who wants me to help him over to America quickly bows over my little American satchel and caresses it vexatiously.

'You work for the Amis!'

'No.'

'Doch!'

There's a hard wind blowing through this station in South Germany. The refugees from the east stamp their feet among their grey bundles. Tired POWs on their way home after years in France saunter to and fro in the cold darkness, woeful men in long French overcoats with a big PG (*prisonnier de guerre*) sewn on the back. On the pillars up and down the platform there are big red WANTED placards describing an escaped Polish murderer, once a guard in a concentration camp, of medium height and armed with a pistol. On the station walls there are other WANTED notices, neatly written ones stuck there by parents seeking children who have disappeared at the front. An astrologer outside Nuremberg promises to trace them in return for twenty marks sent by mail. On big posters a young woman, her skull showing faintly beneath the mask of her face, warns against venereal disease. One has to learn to see death in every woman one meets. A graph demonstrating the incidence of venereal diseases shows an ominous red curve rising at a dreadfully steep angle from July 1945, the month when the soldiers began to feel at home. On the platform opposite ours drunk American boy-soldiers are singing, each one his own hit-song. They fight one another playfully and the smacking sounds of their gloves are like drum-beats in the cold silence. One of them tumbles cursing over a trolley. A couple of staggering girls in their company giggle and cackle in German. Thanksgiving Day.

If I work for the Americans? I explain everything to the boy in the worn-out military coat and cap – a cap of defeat, bashed in and pulled right down over his forehead. He just becomes more eager and reckless and says that I must help him. He looks at the American satchel as if it were a revelation, a victory satchel with full paunch and shining buckles. He bends down over it and tells me about himself. He is sixteen and is called Gerhard. Last night he fled from the Russian zone. Managed to cross the border by train without being stopped. Fled not because the conditions back in Luther's birthplace were particularly intolerable but because he is a mechanic and he

102

did not want to be forced into making a voluntary journey to Russia. So, he has arrived here without money, without anyone he can contact, without even a roof over his head.

'*In Deutschland ist nix mehr los.*' One can't stay in Germany any longer.

I lend him money for a ticket to Hamburg. At least he will get as far as Hamburg; he thinks that ships leave Hamburg for America, ships to hope for. He goes off to buy a ticket and if he wanted to he could easily slip away, refrain from changing the big note and vanish in the darkness outside the station. That would have been normal, more normal than anything else. But the boy who wants to go to America does come back, and when the train reverses in we fight side by side to get places on this cold, pitch-dark train, a typical German post-war train, though with unusually whole windows and with compartments with benches to sit on. Other German trains are dark in the daytime as well because wooden planks have been nailed over the empty window-frames. If you want light you can sit in a compartment without such planks, but it is cold there and the rain comes in.

We are pushed into this nocturnal compartment by busy invisible hands. In the darkness close combat develops, small-scale, quiet, wordless but bitter; trampled children shriek; countless feet kick aside the obstructive bundles of the refugees. The dark compartment is full but it can well be fuller. It is incredible how many people can find space in these miserable square metres. Not until the crush hurts is the door closed; along the train the doors bang shut and we hear the echoing of the despairing voices of those who came too late and now must wait another night among the ruins of this city instead of arriving at the ruins of another one.

We are standing in a compartment with places for eight people but there are twenty-five of us. Twenty-five in a compartment designed for eight – that means it makes no difference if the heat is shut off. Even before the train starts, sweat begins to run. There is no space for two feet, you have to stand on one foot but you do not fall, you hardly need even one foot for even with both feet off the floor you are held in a vice between other sweaty bodies. It is impossible to make one movement without causing someone pain. The lavatories are also full of people, but that matters little – reaching the lavatory is out of the question anyway.

At last the train moves off, the carriages jerk nervously and already the mere fact of finally getting under way brings a certain relief to back, arms and stomach, to everything caught in the vice. We slowly cross the bombed bridge which has very recently – after eighteen months of peace – been meagrely patched up. This is no propaganda bridge of the kind always being opened in German newsreels in the presence of a representative of the military government, a mayor and a pair of scissors that clips through a string and thus, as all the mayors say, helps to increase understanding between Germany and the Allies. Cynical people claim that it is always the same bridge and the same pair of scissors. But different mayors.

The last lights of the city shine in through the window and there in the passing gleam is Gerhard, who, more adept than I am at boarding German trains, has found a window seat. The gleam shows a whole row of tired grey faces: worn-out housewives

104

on their way to the countryside to hunt for potatoes in the villages, prisoners in their greatcoats who have come from Lyons and who say, when the train crosses the bridge so slowly, that since they have waited five years to come home they can also wait through these few hours. Then there are plenty of people without recognized existences: black-marketeers and others who roam from city to city and only God knows what they live off.

We journey on in the thick darkness, sweaty, furious, still not sufficiently exhausted to have given up being irritated. But in this darkness something strange suddenly happens. In Germany there is a kind of emergency pocket-torch whose bottom you have to press repeatedly in order to produce light, a yellow intermittent gleam, and the torch buzzes like a bee while it reluctantly emits its light. Suddenly one of these torches starts buzzing in the darkness down by a bench, and all those whose position will allow them look in its direction and see that it is shining on the palm of a hand, a young woman's hand, and in that hand there lies an apple. A large green juicy apple, one of Germany's biggest. Total silence falls in the compartment, such is the effect of the apple, for apples are rare in Germany. And the apple is simply lying there on the girl's palm, and then the torch goes out and in the breathless silence of the dark there is heard the terribly distinct sound of a bite: the young woman has taken a bite of her apple. The torch buzzes again and there is the apple as before, clearly illuminated on her palm. She directs the beam carefully at the bite, examines the bite; it is a remarkable bite, one that can make you hungry. And how terribly long does that big apple last, and that breathless silence? The young woman with her good teeth, which the whole compartment can feel, shines her torch on the apple each time she has taken a bite, perhaps to demonstrate how easily matter can be defeated.

But by the time the apple has come to an end, apathy has coiled round us. We hang like dead bodies against one another, lean against unknown shoulders and go numb in this suffocating box stinking of sweat and bad air. To keep themselves awake until they change trains the three POWs talk together quietly but with barely restrained vehemence about a cake, a huge and glorious French gateau one of them had eaten in Paris during the occupation. He tries to recall this cake, how deep the layer of cream was, whether it was cognac or arak in that hole in the middle, whether he ate it with a spoon or with a knife or with both.

Towards the end of the night the train stops in a big, empty, brightly illuminated station. There is not one sound to be heard and not one person to be seen. It is like a dream. But suddenly a booming echo reverberates between the station walls: an order is being thrown at us from a loudspeaker. *Passkontrolle. Gepäckkontrolle.* Passport check. Baggage check. The passengers must leave the train, taking their luggage with them. When we have waited for a time on this platform in Eichenberg, a station on the frontier between German England and German America, a few tall American soldiers come along. They chew gum and walk about kicking luggage and examining *Ausweise*. Gerhard is nervous, he has tampered with his passport, contrived to designate himself 'agricultural worker' instead of mechanic in order to cheat

106

the Russians, but all goes well.

From here to Hannover we now stand by a window and talk about his life. He says he is glad that the war went the way it did; he no longer has to go out marching with the Hitler *Jugend* every Sunday, but nevertheless he says that his service in the war was *prima, ganz prima.* He was a mechanic stationed at an airfield in Holland and he claims he will never forget his days there. But now he wants to get away; 'You can't stay in Germany if you're young.'

Before daylight has properly come we watch some dramatic episodes at various stations where we pause. The train is still just as packed as it was, but at those stations there are waiting crowds of despairing people who have as much right to travel as we have. A desperate woman runs along the train and outside every compartment she screams that she must reach a deathbed, but not even someone trying to reach a deathbed can find a place on this train if she lacks the strength to force her way on. A great, rough fellow pushes into our compartment and exchanges blows with a man already standing in the doorway, and since he is a better boxer he thus gets a place on the train. It is the only way.

After Hannover, when many have left the train, there are people standing along the line with full potato-sacks. They drag their sacks over the feet of those who are standing and they smell of earth and autumn. When they heave their sacks up on the luggage racks earth dribbles out over the heads of those sitting beneath. They dry the sweat from their foreheads, both women and men, and they tell us about a tragedy, a potato tragedy, that has just happened.

A woman from Hamburg, who had travelled to Celle with four empty sacks and a handcart and who after four days of relentless effort had managed to fill those sacks through begging from the farmers around Celle, had then by mustering all her strength succeeded in dragging her sacks to the station. When she arrived there her face was glowing with satisfaction. She dried the sweat from her brow, which was then smeared with good earth instead. She had managed. She had done what few others had the ability or the perseverence to do: she had managed to scrape together a whole winter's supply of potatoes for her hungry family. So she stands there in the station at Celle and is pleased with herself and her four days and thinks of the joy that will radiate towards her when she arrives home. She does not yet know that she is a Sisyphus who has rolled her stone up to the hilltop; soon it will tip over and vanish far below. True, she has her sacks and her cart and her strong hands, but her chances of getting into a train are nil. With four potato-sacks no one gets on to a German train. With two perhaps if one can fight. She stands all day waiting for the empty train, the one that will have space for all of her fortune, but such a train does not come, and those with experience tell her that such a train will not come any other day either, such a train will never come at all. She becomes more and more desperate. She must get home at any price; she has already been absent much too long and one cannot walk all the way from Celle to Hamburg. She is now somewhere or other on this train, a bitter and hopelessly tired old woman with one sack of potatoes on the luggage-rack and the other three and a precious handcart in the station at Celle.

The compartment is full of potatoes, the air smells raw and autumnal and everywhere the train stops there are crowds wanting to get on. Someone squeezes in and tells us that now people are sitting on the buffers. Soon we hear the stamping of cold feet above us, so now people are travelling on the roof. It becomes insufferably hot in the compartment. I share my dry sandwiches with Gerhard. Someone pulls the window down and a small hand appears from somewhere outside and grasps the edge of the window, as in a surrealistic film. A boy in front of me questions the reality of that hand, but another boy bets him an Allied cigarette that it is a proper hand. The doubter reaches out his own hand and strokes the unreal one, squeezes it, and it is indeed a real hand. A woman is crouching on the footboard, clinging to the top of the window-pane.

As we cross Lüneburg Heath the first snow of autumn falls and those who clamber down from the roof and in from the buffers and beg to be allowed in are white as cotton. The light fades and some black-marketeers in the compartment exchange cigars and confidences with refined gestures. As we approach Hamburg Gerhard becomes uneasy. His belief in America has now evaporated. America was something he could believe in when Hamburg was twenty-four hours away. He knows there are no boats but he has not yet told himself. Can't he come with me to Sweden? There is nothing I can say to that. All I can do is stare up at the muddy potato-sacks, keep silent and suffer a bad conscience.

We come into Hamburg almost four hours late or, as it is called in the language of inflation, two hundred and thirty minutes. It is cold and windy and it is snowing. The snow is falling on the ruins and on the dirty piles of bricks and on the girls from the Reeperbahn who are hungry for food but not for love. The snow is falling on the sluggish canals where sunk barges lie at rest under a roof of greasy oil. We walk for a while in the cold, Gerhard and I. Then we have to part outside the hotel with the sign NO GERMAN CIVILIANS. I shall go through the swing-door and enter a dining-room with glasses and white table-cloths and a gallery where in the evening musicians play from the *Tales of Hoffmann*. I shall sleep in a soft bed in a warm room with hot and cold running water. But Gerhard Blume walks on, out in Hamburg's night. He does not even go to the harbour. And nothing can be done about that. Absolutely nothing.

Literature and Suffering

What is the distance between literature and suffering? Does it depend on the nature of the suffering, on its closeness or on its strength? Is the distance less between poetry and the suffering caused by the reflection of the fire than the distance between poetry and the suffering arising from the fire itself? There are examples to hand that show there is a more or less immediate connection between poetry and remote or closed suffering. Perhaps we can say that simply to suffer with others is a form of poetry, which feels a powerful longing for words. Immediate open suffering distinguishes itself from the indirect kind by, among other things, not longing for words, at least not at the moment it occurs. Open suffering is shy, restrained, taciturn.

As the plane rises towards the winter evening in a cloud of German rain and German snow, as the surviving German eagle on the airport vanishes in the gloom beneath us, while the lights of Frankfurt are extinguished in the smothering dark and the Swedish plane climbs above German suffering at a speed of 300 kilometres an hour, there is perhaps one question more than any other weighing on the traveller: What

111

would it be like to have to stay behind, to have to be hungry every day, to have to sleep in a cellar, to fight at every moment against the temptation to steal, to have to tremble with cold every minute, to have to survive, constantly, the most intractable conditions? I remember people I met who had to tolerate almost all of that. And I remember above all certain poets and artists – they were not hungrier or suffering more than others, but I remember them because they were aware of the possibilities of suffering, they had tried to measure the distance between art and suffering.

One day in the Ruhr when it has been raining endlessly and when the bakers have not had bread for two days I meet a young German author, one of those who came out during the war but on account of certain spiritual reserves cannot be said personally to have 'lost a war'. He has been allowed to borrow a fine Swiss-style villa in the middle of a forest and several kilometres of flaming red trees separate him from the most brutal privations of the brutally deprived Ruhr. It is strange to come from the lower depths of a Ruhr mine where a despairing miner with bloodshot eyes in a black face pulled off his battered shoes to let me see he had no socks – to come from there right into this autumnal idyll where hunger and cold were themselves cultivated to the point where they acquired almost ritualistic dimensions. It is a strange experience even to walk in an unspoiled garden, and in this bookless Germany, where a book is such a rarity that one approaches it with reverence simply because it is a book, to step into a room overflowing with books, from Dante's *Inferno* to Strindberg's.

On this island in a terrible sea sits a young author with the tired smile and the aristocratic name, smoking cigarettes for which he has traded away books, drinking tea whose taste is as bitter as the autumn outside. His way of life is certainly peculiar. The outer world, which consists of starving miners, grey tenements with ruined façades and grey cellar-people whose rickety air-raid-shelter beds stand in ankle-deep water when it rains as it is raining now – this world is not unknown here but it is not accepted – it is held at the distance which objectionable things deserve. Personally he is quite uninterested in what is happening a few kilometres away: his wife, who goes to the village for provisions, and the children, who travel to school by train, constitute his only, tranquil contact with life and death out there. Just now and then, and as seldom as possible, does he leave the lonely house in the rainy garden and venture out into the repugnant reality, with the same reluctance with which the hermits of the desert would make their way towards the oasis.

But even a hermit must live. Germany's authors, who cannot have books published except through lucky accident, live mainly by travelling around giving readings or lectures: these are long, chilly and depressing expeditions from which one returns full of the cold, exhausted and quite unable to write. No one becomes rich doing this – it does not even produce enough to make ends meet. If one has books they must be sold off for tea or sugar or cigarettes. If one has more typewriters than necessary they can be bartered for paper, and if the author wants pens to write with he can get them by trading away his dearly acquired paper.

My hermit friend gives lectures on Möricke and Burckhardt, his two timeless favourites. He gave the same lectures to French-German gatherings in occupied France from Paris to Bordeaux. He says thoughtfully that that was his best time and he claims that people listened better there, that the climate was more favourable for German lectures in occupied France beteen 1940 and 1944 than in the devastated Ruhr of 1946. Of course, he says, I was aware of the situation, but why should a military necessity prevent me from contributing towards mutual understanding between German and French culture? It sounds cynical until one gets used to it, and the reality was in fact even more cynical. On his shelves I come across two dainty army editions, one of the poems of Hölderlin and one of the poems of Möricke, printed in 1941. We can imagine that German soldiers with Möricke's poems in their inside pockets subjugated Greece, or that after yet another Russian village had been levelled to the ground the German soldier returned to his interrupted reading of Hölderlin, the German poet who said of love that it conquers both time and bodily death.

But there is a satisfactory answer to all questions. Cruelty can be explained by saying that war has its own laws. It is not cynicism when this author says that in spite of everything he admired the French Resistance – all resistance movements indeed, except for the German one because that did not have a national foundation.

'It was only those who couldn't keep their mouths shut who landed up in concentration camps. Why couldn't people just hold their tongues and survive these twelve years?'

114

'How did you know at the time that it would be twelve years?'

'It could have been more. Of course. But then what? Why not see this too in a historical perspective, why not judge what has happened as if it had happened a hundred years ago? Strictly speaking reality doesn't begin to exist until the historian has put it into its context and then it's too late to experience it, and vex over it, or weep. To be real, reality must be old.'

Right enough, in this room in a villa in the Ruhr reality does not exist. True, in the course of the afternoon, the wife comes into the room crying and tells us about a scene that has just taken place in the bakery. A man with a big stick had forced his way past terror-stricken, waiting women and seized the last loaf without anyone in the queue managing to prevent him. But for the born classicist the intermezzo is hardly painful enough to force the regrettable reality, taking place right now, into his life. We sit in the gathering dark and talk about the baroque, the whole room is full of the baroque: on the table there are thick German theses on the baroque as a building-style. He is in the course of writing a novel set in the baroque era and based on an uncompleted project of von Hofmannsthal: that is why he is now reading everything he can about baroque architecture, to be able to construct a true reality for his characters, who will not be thinly disguised contemporaries with bread shortages and hunger obsessions, but proper baroque people of baroque flesh and baroque blood, thinking baroque thoughts and living baroque lives. Baroque – hardly, one would think, an up-to-date way of living in a Ruhr on the verge of hunger-riots.

But up to date? In this literary workshop where time does not exist until it is too late?

But where is the root of suffering? He begins talking about the happiness of suffering, about the beauty of suffering. Suffering is not dirty, suffering is not pitiable. No, suffering is great because suffering makes people great. 'What accounts for the conquests of the old German culture? The fact that the German people had to suffer more than other peoples!' It is impossible to convince him that suffering is something unworthy. The romantic historian in him acknowledges suffering as the most powerful driving-force behind great human endeavours, and to the born classicist it is the driving-force behind great literature, which does not necessarily need to be literature about suffering.

At the dinner-table his mother, whose aristocratic pallor is a product of equal parts nobility and undernourishment, talks with the same pleasurable joy about the happiness of German suffering. We eat potatoes and kale because at the moment there is nothing else to eat, and the various members of the family urge one another to take a little more although the urging is strictly ironic. In this highly cultivated family hunger is put to use as a stimulant. The meal acquires a special significance because it is the second-last typewriter which is being eaten up. I eat little, at the most one key or two. Then the author returns to the last typewriter and the baroque, which he has never left, and I set out into the Ruhr which is as little baroque as possible. In the garden I meet the two schoolgirls on their way home: Maresi, christened after a story by Lernet-Holenia, and Victoria, named after the defeat of France in 1940, children who are

116

pale chiefly from undernourishment. But as the car drives back through Düsseldorf it is a chubby baroque angel I seem to see displaying his ghostly wings against the darkening ruins.

One month later, in Hannover, in a painter's studio. We talk about the collapse and about the new German art. I have seen some strangely bland exhibitions. The most interesting perhaps was one by a group of idealistically Communist artists, remarkable not as art but as propaganda. In a beautifully scripted display-programme they announce their devotion to the reorganization of the world into a huge trade union. All the social units we know at present are to be replaced by compounds with the word *Werk*—. We shall no longer talk about artists but about *Werkleute*, not about studios but about *Werkstätte*, not about nations but about *Gewerkschaften*. And so on. There was also a programmatic ruin – a quite unrealistic stage-set ruin in the background, in front of which were two playing children and flowers. Bad theatre – nothing else. At another exhibition the commonest motif was not ruins but the heads of smashed classical statues lying on the ground with the Mona-Lisa smile of defeat.

'But when I paint ruins,' says the painter in Hannover, 'I do that because I think they are beautiful and not because they are ruins. There are masses of ugly houses which have become things of beauty after the bombing. The museum in Hannover really looks quite passable as a ruin, especially when the sun breaks through the shattered roof.'

Suddenly he grasps my arm. We look out on the shabby street. A black procession of nuns, one of the world's most proper sights, shows up against one of

117

the most improper: a lewd ruin with clinging pipes and gallows-like rafters.

'I'll paint that some day, not because it is a ruin but because the contrast is *so verdammt erschütternd.*'

Berlin, 3 February 1945, during a raid. That is a date in a chapter from a novel, published in a German magazine and one of the few instances of a young German writer coming to grips with the recently terminated suffering. It describes a tram-conductor's last afternoon. He arrives home to find the house empty at an unusual time. His daughter is epileptic and anything may have happened. As a huge American raid closes in on Berlin the tram-conductor, Max Eckert, sets off on a terrible odyssey which ends at the underground station where his family in all probability were burnt beyond recognition together with thousands of others. In a fit of rage he attacks a policeman who greets him with '*Heil Hitler*' and he is shot. It is a grim and chilling extract from a novel in progress, *Finale Berlin*, which turns out to be a collective novel of suffering, an interpretation of the terrible suffering of the bombed, a suffering which is common property to every German city-dweller and still lives in the senses as bitterness, as hysteria, as repugnance, as lovelessness.

Meanwhile the Swedish plane has climbed still higher over the German plight. We fly above white evening clouds and there are old-fashioned ice-ferns on the windows. But about three thousand metres under us, at a sharp angle now, there is a woman living only in order to write a big novel about another kind of suffering: that of the concentration camp prisoners. She has herself spent several years in a camp for

118

political offenders. In that camp she belonged to the so-called Rilke Group, a small fanatical group of women who during the breaks and in danger of their lives would gather in a corner of the compound and in whispers read the poems of Rilke to one another. But it is not her own suffering she wants to write about, she wants to write about a suffering that was greater: her husband's. He spent eight years in Dachau and is now an old man twenty years before his time: white-haired, tottering, hoarse. Now she is trying to train him to speak: in the evenings before they go to sleep, through the night when they lie awake, at meal-times; but he does not understand her, he does not understand how she should want to write about what he has suffered. And none of their friends and acquaintances understand either, not him who has just come back from a Russian camp and in sharp contrast to most home-comers has become enthusiastically pro-Russian on account of the fact that he was not shot the moment he was captured. He was taken at Stalingrad and now he never tires of relating how he and his fellow soldiers once festooned the railings of a bridge with naked Russian corpses for the fun of getting a unique snapshot. He will never come to understand that he was allowed to survive. The practical, extrovert Anny, who spent three years in political detention and who has just returned from a three-day 200-kilometre journey for a sack of potatoes, he does not understand either.

But the woman who wants to write says bitterly that in the course of a year she has been able to find out only the following about her husband's sufferings: During the night someone has fled, and at dawn all the prisoners are lined up and made to stand at

119

attention in the pouring rain all day and the next night and all the next day. Those who cannot hold out are lost. At the time when they normally get their food the escapee is brought back, the guards strap a huge drum on him and for the rest of the day he is made to parade up and down before his comrades, drumming a march, endlessly the same march, his own death-march. At midnight he collapses and that is the last they see of him.

It is a dreadful episode but it is not enough for a book and she never learns more. The suffering is suffered and then it should not exist any longer. This suffering was grubby, offensive, mean and small, and therefore one should not speak or write about it. There is too short a distance between writing and the worst kind of suffering; it is only when the suffering has become a cleansed memory that the time may be right. And yet she goes on hoping, each time she is alone with him she hopes to hear those words which will give her the strength to dip her pen in suffering.

Three thousand five hundred metres. The ice-ferns thicken on the windows. The moon has risen, a frosty ring round it. We are told of our whereabouts. We are flying over Bremen but Bremen is not to be seen. Lacerated Bremen is lying hidden beneath dense German clouds, as impenetrably hidden as the mute German agony. We fly out over the sea and on this rolling, marbly floor of clouds and moonlight we take leave of Germany, autumnal and icebound.

Stig Dagerman (1923–1954) was regarded as the most talented writer of the Swedish postwar generation. He published his first novel, *The Snake*, at age twenty-two, and within four years he wrote four novels, a collection of short stories, a considerable volume of journalism, and four full-length plays. He was at the forefront of Swedish letters in the 1940s, with critics comparing him to William Faulkner, Franz Kafka, and Albert Camus. He died at age thirty-one.

Mark Kurlansky is the *New York Times* best-selling author of many books, including *Cod: A Biography of the Fish That Changed the World; Salt: A World History; Nonviolence: Twenty-five Lessons from the History of a Dangerous Idea;* and *A Chosen Few: The Resurrection of European Jewry.* He lives in New York City and writes frequently about Germany.

Robin Fulton Macpherson is a Scottish poet and translator who has lived in Norway since 1973. He has translated the work of several Swedish poets.

CPSIA information can be obtained
at www.ICGtesting.com
Printed in the USA
JSHW021057171222
35000JS00007B/181

9 780816 677528